Learning to Belong

Building on highly topical research surrounding young children's participation, this book draws from a diversity of disciplines to explore the importance of participatory approaches to children's early education and show how fostering a sense of identity and belonging is essential to early learning.

Taking young children seriously demands a high level of confidence and leadership from early years practitioners. The author provides a convincing, well-researched rationale for using this approach in early years contexts. Chapters in this book:

- demonstrate the importance of listening to the voices of the children;
- show how to help young children make sense of the rules and hierarchies they encounter in the classroom;
- explore ways of working that include young children but also allow adults to shape approaches to collective decision-making;
- use examples of the type of questions children might ask when they first enter school, which are presented as 'windows' into children's experiences via key moments or incidents in the school day;
- provide a framework and practical tools for planning.

Learning to Belong is an important addition to the debate about the politics and ethics of a highly prescribed, and mainly developmentally informed, early years curriculum. Researchers and students of early childhood education will find much here of interest to them.

Caroline Bath is Senior Lecturer in Early Childhood Studies at Sheffield Hallam University.

Learning to Belong

Exploring young children's participation
at the start of school

Caroline Bath

Routledge
Taylor & Francis Group

LONDON AND NEW YORK

First published 2009
by Routledge
2 Park Square, Milton Park, Abingdon, Oxon OX14 4RN

Simultaneously published in the USA and Canada
by Routledge
270 Madison Avenue, New York, NY 10016

Routledge is an imprint of the Taylor & Francis Group, an informa business

© 2009 Caroline Bath

Typeset in Garamond by
GreenGate Publishing Services, Tonbridge, Kent
Printed and bound in Great Britain by
CPI Antony Rowe, Chippenham, Wiltshire

All rights reserved. No part of this book may be reprinted or
reproduced or utilised in any form or by any electronic, mechanical,
or other means, now known or hereafter invented, including
photocopying and recording, or in any information storage or
retrieval system, without permission in writing from the publishers.

British Library Cataloguing in Publication Data
A catalogue record for this book is available from the British Library

Library of Congress Cataloging-in-Publication Data
Bath, Caroline, 1958-
Learning to belong : exploring young children's participation at the start of
school / Caroline Bath.
p. cm.
Includes bibliographical references and index.|
1. Early childhood education. 2. Active learning. I. Title.
LB1139.23.B38 2009
372.21--dc22
2008042401

ISBN 10: 0-415-48366-2 (hbk)
ISBN 10: 0-415-48368-9 (pbk)
ISBN 10: 0-203-87982-1 (ebk)

ISBN 13: 978-0-415-48366-7 (hbk)
ISBN 13: 978-0-415-48368-1 (pbk)
ISBN 13: 978-0-203-87982-5 (ebk)

For Sybil Bath, my mother and first teacher

Contents

Figures and tables

Figures

Tables

Acknowledgements

With thanks to the teachers and children who participated in the project and to Mark Gibson, colleagues and friends who supported me along the way.

Note on the text

All the names of teachers and children in this book have been changed to ensure anonymity.

Introduction

The stranger is thus being discussed here, not in the sense often touched upon in the past, as the wanderer who comes today and goes tomorrow, but rather as the person who comes today and stays to morrow ... He is fixed within a particular spatial group, or within a group whose boundaries are similar to spatial boundaries. But his position in this group is determined, essentially, by the fact that he has not belonged to it from the beginning, that he imports qualities into it, which do not and cannot stem from the group itself.

> (Georg Simmel (1950) 'The stranger' in Kurt Wolff (trans.)
> *The Sociology of Georg Simmel*)

A sense of belonging is difficult to define yet also fundamental to the well-being of members of a community. It infers what underpins community membership: a social and emotional commitment which connects with individual agency. This book aims to explore how the concept of belonging relates to young children starting the statutory school system in England. These children enter the school community in the same position as the 'stranger', described above, and, like Simmel's stranger, often learn the art of adaptation searchingly, if somewhat painfully. Moreover, this perspective on children starting school suggests that there is value in standing outside while also learning to be inside. This is a point to savour and remember. In other words, communities benefit from the critical processes of questioning and dialogue which those who are learning to belong bring with them. In brief, young children starting school have much to offer to the process of their induction.

This period of transition for young children, from stranger to that of belonging to a school community, has been examined variously as a time of 'learning cultures' (Brooker, 2002) and 'a major challenge of early childhood' (Fabian and Dunlop, 2006, p.2). It has also been seen as a process which involves all the 'stakeholders', including children (Dockett and Perry, 2005). International interest in the theme has grown, particularly in Australia

(Dockett and Perry, 2005) and Scandinavia (Einarsdottir, 2006) and particular attention has been paid by several of these researchers to children from culturally and linguistically diverse backgrounds, for whom starting school may be an even more complex transition. Dockett and Perry (2005, p.272), for instance, talk about children experiencing 'confusion' as a result of 'home–school inconsistencies'. The origin for this confusion is identified as an unconnectedness between school and families which can arise from either differences in culture or expectations of home and school. Since this experience of transition alienates both families and children from school, Dockett and Perry (2005, p.272) suggest that 'a sense of belonging' is a vital part of adjusting well to school, a sentiment frequently asserted as imperative for successful transition experiences in many different situations for children and adults alike.

In early childhood education, the concept of belonging has most notably been embraced in the early years *Te Whaariki* curriculum of New Zealand, which has embedded the concept of belonging. Although this will be returned to in later chapters, it is worth noting at this point that the basis for *Te Whaariki* lies in a sociocultural approach to curriculum which is widely regarded as progressive. Thus, the strand of 'belonging', which is included as one of five curriculum strands, relies on a view of human development as grounded in an ecological model derived from Bronfenbrenner (1979). This model emphasises responsive learning contexts and reciprocal interaction and also lends itself to the notion that children's learning is situated within family and cultural contexts, rather than that of developmental psychology. Thus, Carr and May (2000) suggest that 'the child's question', which arises in relation to the strand of belonging, is: 'Do you appreciate and understand my interests and abilities and those of my family?' In other words, 'Do you know me?' Clearly, therefore, as an early years curriculum, *Te Whaariki* is significant for taking an approach which policy and practice for children's transition to school could do to adopt.

However, whilst many investigations have focused on the initial impact for children and parents of entering a new and potentially alien environment, less attention has been paid to the pedagogical work of the teacher as children's first year at school progresses. Therefore the main purpose of this book is to suggest that this crucial aspect should be given due importance and substance. Since children's journey of belonging regularly crosses borders between home and school and is important beyond the first few weeks at school, the teacher has a significant role during this first year in the classroom, of recognising and addressing possible alienation. Thus, the extent to which membership of a school community has been achieved at the end of the initial year is best measured by the extent to which children's, parents' and teacher's interpretations of settling in find common ground.

Children are not, of course, homogenous and do not all interpret things in the same way. Nevertheless, children starting school are subject to similar cultural expectations which surround significant markers of growth in a person's life. Prout and James (1997, p.7) capture this well when they allude to La Fontaine (1979) and say that 'the immaturity of children is a biological fact of life but the ways in which this immaturity is understood and made meaningful is a fact of culture'. Furthermore, Prout and James (1997) state that transition points in childhood 'are strategic points for analysis, allowing the focus on the present of childhood ... whilst at the same time maintaining firm links with the past and future of the life courses on which children are embarked' (p.249). They make the case that these emblematic times resonate with the emerging paradigm for the sociology of childhood in that '"time in childhood"' (p.231) is accorded such significance. In this paradigm of childhood sociology, children are studied 'not only as proto-adults... but as beings-in-the-present' (p.245). Thus, children are taken seriously and differences between them acknowledged as part of a continuum of difference in society.

Therefore, this book argues that the transition issue we should concentrate on is the one that occurs in the process of children communicating and understanding concepts of belonging. Clearly, moving into a new environment and adopting different daily routines increases pressure on children to develop new and shared understandings of the world but this pressure may be positively or negatively handled by those in control. Although one meaning of 'to belong' is 'to be in the right place' the 'rightness' of a place depends not only on physical space but also on relationships and routines and it is through the negotiation of these, in the context of adults and peers in the classroom, that children find membership of a school community.

The other associated theme of this book is the conjunction between ideas and practices which suggest that teachers and other practitioners should constantly reflect upon and question what they do and the messages that practice transmits to the children in their care. The power of practice to contain ideas is expressed by Paulo Freire's idea of 'praxis' which suggests that reflection and action upon the world effects transformation (Freire, 1970). Furthermore, Freire says that praxis is fundamental to both human life and the possibility of freedom. Thus he suggests that, through action, people shape history and culture, at the same time as being subjected to their constraints. Praxis, therefore, is integral to Freire's theoretical constructs and education is centrally positioned as the practice of the freedom which praxis allows (Glass, 2001). As Williams (1958) also says: 'we begin to think where we live'.

Following Freire's ideas, I contend that the practices that young children experience in school inform the most powerful lessons they learn and that, importantly, these 'lessons' are often outside the visible curriculum and are embedded in attitudes and values signalled by those practices. These are difficult to define but, nevertheless, it is these attitudes and values which teachers and practitioners working with children should examine and reflect upon when they plan activities and ways of working. Freire's notion of praxis makes untenable a division between theory and practice in the field of education and this book aims to cross the rift which such a division causes. The central principle which such a crossing is based upon is one which upholds reflection as an essential practitioner quality. To stretch this further, I would also suggest that, in this context, reflection needs to be framed by attention to the ideas of social justice and diversity which underpin the substance of this book.

Chapter 1

Planning the project

Theory and practice in the classroom

In order to examine the theme of belonging in relation to children at the start of school, this book will recount the setting up, carrying out and findings of a research project undertaken in 2003–4. In this chapter, I will look at the planning that went into the project, in terms of the theoretical approaches, methods and practical arrangements that informed the study. It is important to note that the research arose out of professional concerns and disquiet, which are recounted in the next chapter, and also that it was carried out in the context of the classroom.

Following the influence of Freire (1970), as previously outlined in the introduction to this book, I hoped to articulate that at the heart of teaching is a practice that finds its roots in the performance of thought. This suggests that the theory that matters can and should find its way into the classroom through the medium of communication that exists between the teacher and the pupil. If we accept that ideas do not exist independently of the practices that beget them, so big ideas can be expressed in the smallest of places and there should be no need to look outside of an early years classroom for inspiration. However, this is not to say that you need only look inside the classroom for inspiration. What matters, I believe, are the links between ideas and the spaces where these ideas are extracted and enacted. It is, therefore, the seamless connections which the teacher performs between the world of thought and the social world of the classroom which transform this environment into an educational one. This perspective places communication and learning at the centre of teaching and suggests that the pupil must have equal involvement in this two-way process, which by inference rests on a democratic view of pedagogy.

Whilst planning the research project, experience of studying other disciplines, and in particular political and literary theory, had demonstrated to me that links can be made in all directions and that compartmentalisation, both between subjects and between notions of theory and practice, or 'academic' and 'vocational', is a social construct that needs dismantling to bring dynamism into our social life. Thus, my contention was that this dynamism can be conceived of as the education-in-practice that can change children's lives by broadening possibilities and suggesting alternatives to them. Teachers have a vital role in bringing this about and need opportunities for pedagogical support and development to help them to perform it.

As a teacher myself, I felt strongly that classroom research needed the involvement of theoretical and practical knowledge in equal measure. This meant that the research had to be grounded in everyday practice and also benefit that practice. I had had experience of researchers coming into classrooms to 'do' research and saw this as a difficult and potentially intrusive model of research which was often modelled on research designs that did not feed back directly to the classroom research participants. It was important, therefore, that the subject of the research, which was derived from questions and concerns about my own practice and in particular, children's sense of belonging in the classroom, was articulated as political in both form and content. Thus, the subject of the research, which will be expanded upon in the next chapter, became 'young children's participation'. Using this theme, I aimed to explore how children's sense of belonging is constructed, supported and learnt. This was, by implication, a theme which demanded a model of research involving consultation with the participants during the planning and modification of the research design. Perhaps, most importantly, it also involved the class teacher as the central player on the research field and demanded a high level of researcher reflexivity, to navigate the ethical dimension of the relationships which were intrinsic to the research.

However, this outlook immediately created dilemmas for the research, because my position as a teacher in the project, which will discussed more fully in chapter four, was as an early years support teacher, employed by the local education authority to support the inclusion of children with special educational needs in the classroom. Therefore, I was a step removed from a class teacher's direct and ongoing relationship with a whole group of children. Consequently, it was important for the research that I considered how to facilitate close collaboration with the class teachers who wanted to encourage pupil participation and actively engage with research themselves. The research design also had to enable me to build a consistent role with the children in their classes.

Therefore, to gain the co-operation of class teachers, I wrote to all the schools in the city to ask for volunteers who had the experience and support of their schools to develop participatory practices. I then visited and spoke to all the respondents. In the spirit of the research itself, eventually the research participants chose themselves and subject to support from their head teachers and the logistics of their schools' distance from my usual area of work, three volunteers emerged. They covered a range of types of school, representative of varying socio-economic areas, size of school and foundation stage unit which are outlined below.

The schools

The project which is discussed throughout this book took place in three different reception class settings (now commonly referred to as Foundation 2 classes) in a northern city in England. The three schools (hereafter referred to as Allen Road, St Bedes and Cooper Street) represented some variation which, though secondary to the main criteria of the teachers' interest in the project, nevertheless enabled useful comparisons to be made. The following provides some of the relevant features of each school and corresponding reception class teacher.

Allen Road School was a primary school in an area of extensive council housing and high levels of social deprivation and unemployment, within one of the poorest wards in the country. The school had two classes in each year and a 52-place nursery. This school had been in special measures in recent years but had made excellent progress under a former head teacher in reaching the standards required. The pupils were mainly white with little ethnic diversity. The Allen Road reception class teacher was an experienced class teacher who had 20 pupils in her class with one full-time nursery nurse to assist her. Under the new head teacher, early years issues had gained prominence and she was able to try new ways of working in accordance with the foundation stage curriculum guidance (DfEE, 2000).

St Bedes Infant School, in contrast, was a small school in a rural area on the outskirts of the city. This area was mixed economically but had predominantly private housing. The school had one class in each year and no nursery, though an array of local private and voluntary pre-school providers. The school enjoyed a good reputation in the local community for the standards set. The pupils were almost entirely white with very little ethnic diversity. The St Bedes reception class teacher was more experienced with older infant children and was new to reception age children. She had recently spent time out of teaching to raise a family. She had 30 pupils in her class with a part-time assistant.

Cooper Street Primary School was on the opposite side of the city to the other two schools. It was a large, Victorian-built school, with two classes in each year and included a 52-place nursery. It was within an area of high social deprivation with mixed housing and broad ethnic diversity. The school was in special measures with an acting head teacher. The Cooper Street reception class teacher was in her second year of teaching reception age children. She had previously worked with a variety of age groups and had spent several years teaching abroad. She had 18 children in her class with a part-time assistant and was due to expand the class by six children in the second term.

The aims and questions

At the outset of the research, it was important to conceptualise aims. In the case of this project, these were part of the process of making the research tangible to both the participants and my employer who supported me. They were articulated in this way:

- To develop an understanding of what participation means in the context of the reception class by working with three class teachers to analyse and develop their existing practices in the light of inclusive aims.
- To develop and assess strategies for the participation of young children in a reception class setting.
- To explore the development of young children's potential to make and conceptualise collective decisions.

In order to achieve these aims, the questions that I wished to pose initially were:

- What are the features in reception class practice that encourage young children's decision-making and participation?
- How can young children learn to participate at the start of school?

The approaches

Participatory action research

Given my belief in the connection between experience and theory which led me to this research, it was unsurprising that the first methodological approach that I worked from was an approach of 'action research'. Thereby, I intended to improve my own practices as an early years teacher and work with other teachers to do the same.

The emphasis on practices and their outcomes provides a moral purpose to action research and also a radical view of educational theory which then becomes grounded in practical reality. Carr and Kemmis (1986) note that there is a 'double dialectic' at work in their model of action research which enables theory to confront practice and also the individual to confront society. The resolution of these opposing forces is to be found in the notion of a self-critical community of action researchers 'committed to the improvement of education' (p.184). This model suggests a transformation of practice into 'praxis' (p.190) through the creation of research as a critical educational science. Meanwhile, as Lather points out, 'the question of action remains largely under-addressed within postmodern discourse' (1991, p.12).

Research into participation as a political subject linked to democracy suggests a critical examination of the discrimination which exists in the classroom, as it does in society. However, it is also necessarily a subject that derives from and builds on everyday classroom practices, rather than from a discrete theoretical category. This is recognised in guidance for teachers such as the *Index for Inclusion* (Booth *et al.*, 2000), which includes a checklist against which teachers can assess their inclusive and 'participatory' practices. However, my concern was that this document could be interpreted as a catechism of possible fault, blame and hope, rather than allowing practitioners to take centre stage in devising their own interpretations of participation and inclusion in their classrooms. Therefore, following the notion of action research as a critical educational science, the project aimed to place the creative and critical faculties of the practitioner at the centre, by looking at practices developed through ongoing dialogue with the other participants in classroom life. In this scenario there is commitment to discourse and the improvement of education but no single text to follow.

Carr and Kemmis (1986) emphasise that when a practical activity such as teaching is under the spotlight, then a different view of knowledge is needed than the 'single sphere of "theoria" which in the Greek tradition was reserved for the contemplation of ultimate truths' (p.99). They also suggest that educational problems occur when there are gaps between a practitioner's theory and practice (p.112). It is therefore vital that practitioners are able to exercise rational and coherent judgments which lend scientific objectivity to the development of their practices and recreate theory as a more embodied force. Ultimately Carr and Kemmis (1986) feel that truth and action are interdependent and exist together socially in the midst of constructed meanings within a historical context. This view gives us some certainty as well as flexibility and frees us up as practitioners to challenge a hierarchy of knowledge that excludes the reality of the grass roots. By following this approach, Carr and Kemmis's notion of a critical social science aims to clarify, explain and eliminate 'the causes of distorted self-understanding' (1986, p.174). In this way, a theoretical understanding may also underpin and illuminate our interpretations. Importantly, a critical social theory 'arises out of the problems of everyday life and is constructed with an eye towards solving them' (p.175). It focuses on the collective and also aims to be useful.

Because this project formed part of my ongoing teaching role as a support teacher, there was inevitability to its action research methodology. A process of reflection and interpretation by practitioners was viewed as one which support teachers could facilitate in a structured way as part of their role to advocate participation in schools. This is explored further in chapter four by looking at the role of the researcher and teacher in the research.

Since the research questions were also overtly engaged with the subject of participation, in order to further tie together subject and method, my intention was to take the research beyond action research and into a more conscious form of participatory action research. This type of research, say Kemmis and McTaggart (2000, p.569), has roots in liberation theology, neo-Marxist approaches to community development and human rights activism. The advantage of Kemmis and McTaggart's view of participatory action research is that it not only provides an opportunity for the researcher to become an insider and thus gain inside knowledge, but also makes possible 'the seed of the critical perspective' (2000, p.590) so that other possibilities and views are considered. This means that the participants inevitably embark on a process of self-education and commitment to change.

The strength of the participatory approach to research for this project was the interlinking of both agency and structure which meant that education was a central theme in the methodology. This allowed some perspective without losing the power of the fieldwork context and it is further explored, in terms of its implications for practical application to the project, in chapter four.

Ethnography

What was at stake in this project was what happens in the classroom on a daily basis. It therefore seemed appropriate to characterise this project not just as participatory action research but also as ethnography based on participant observation. This allowed for the research method to reflect another aspect of the subject matter, by centring on the interactions in the classroom. In this way, it encapsulated the process of interpretation itself, since communication cuts across participation and also elicits contradiction. Thus, the accounts of class teachers and children as co-researchers were seen as central and attempts were made to capture their original expression. These accounts were also shaped by my own writing and thoughts which were recorded in a weekly research journal.

Ethnography literally means the writing of a culture. It is a broad canvas that has been reworked to accommodate postmodernity and feminist politics so that, as Tedlock (2000) points out, 'an ethnographer can allow self and other to appear together within a single narrative that carries a multiplicity of dialoguing voices' (p.471). This means that the emancipatory dimension of a project which prioritises participation can be well accommodated within the ethnographic frame. As Denzin (2000) says, the interpretive criteria of qualitative research are now pushing 'the personal to the forefront of the political, where the social text becomes the vehicle for the expression of politics' (p.915). This perspective adds an edge of activism to the postmodernist flavour of interpretive methodology.

Perhaps with this in mind, Denzin (1997) also suggests that ethnography should move closer to a type of civic journalism that 'makes readers actors and participants, not spectators' (p.280). The text which this type of ethnography incurs is described by Marcus (1994) as 'messy text'. This is representation which is closer to the research process itself than to a finished product or artefact. Denzin (1997) points out that, by attempting to reflexively map multiple discourses, these texts suggest poststructural readings for which 'no interpretation is privileged' (p.225). These then 'redirect ethnography towards constructing itself as social criticism, rather than as social science' (p.232).

To summarise the approaches taken to the research, the theoretical approaches drew from methodologies which have often been characterised as contradictory. However, the development of action research as participatory and the use of ethnography as critical, in my view, allowed these approaches to work together to represent diverse and often confusing voices in order to shape future practices. It is also relevant to point out that, far from being inflexible, ethnography can be seen as 'a hybrid textual activity' that 'traverse genres and disciplines' (Clifford, 1986, p.26). Thus, producing ethnography presupposes the essentially active process of getting one's hands dirty in a chosen field of work. Schon (1983) likens this to being in a swamp wherein 'lie the problems of greatest human concern' (p.3). Anthropology, sociology and literary criticism are but a few of the disciplines which ethnography touches, making a 'politics of location' (Marcus, 1994, p.570) all the more important to its sense of identity as fieldwork.

Whilst the representation of the research attempted to make sense of 'messy text' through an ethnographic approach, nevertheless there were also other dimensions of the representative process to consider. For instance, it was also important to the overall spirit of its theme that the presentation of findings to other teachers and researchers allowed for ongoing dissemination and reinterpretation of the fieldwork before the final version was written. Additionally, future representations of the findings were also a possibility in the light of further writing and research experience of the author. Furthermore, the use of story in narrative techniques for engaging children in debate was utilised as a method and is discussed later.

The methods

In order to carry out the approaches detailed above, the outline methods for exploring the research questions (p.7) were planned as:

- an analysis of the classroom organisation and teaching techniques which promote children's participation through participant observation of and collaboration with three reception class teachers in three separate schools;
- observations of and transcripts of conversations about participation with children in each class, including a particular focus on one child in each class;
- activities and 'techniques' to explore and promote children's participation with reference to participatory rural appraisal (PRA) techniques;
- questionnaire feedback from the participant teachers;
- four visits each term to each setting over one academic year (total of twelve visits each) including individual teacher consultation sessions;
- one joint meeting for teachers per term over one academic year (three altogether).

The practice of written participant observation is part of an accepted technique in educational research. Denscombe (1998) suggests that it can provide ways of 'gaining rich insights into social processes' as well as the actors' meanings 'as they see them' (p.156). Clearly there is a naturalness associated with this method that adds authenticity and validity to the research process, but the hazard of deception may also be incurred. Working alongside the class teachers in this project at times blurred the research and the classroom agenda. If the project were to be repeated, I would aim for the collaborative work with teachers to incur greater problematisation and thus become even more central to the research.

Arguably, although parents had given consent on their children's behalf, the initial focus on teaching practices acted to prevent clear assent being given by the children to participate in the research project. Children were asked whether they wanted to take part in activities and were able to refuse, though it would be fair to say that they were not necessarily fully aware of the purposes of the work. Clearly, a future study focusing on young children's participation would need to plan for a significant amount of time and space in order to gain (or not gain) children's assent to take part in research.

The other issue which is exacerbated by the use of participant observation is the nature of selective recall and perception. Whilst the use of a digital tape recorder helped to record actual conversations with children, observations were often written after the visit and shaped by the experience of the visit. This highlights the interpretive nature of observation and, therefore, can be justified as a strength and integral part of ethnographic representation. However, the reflexive researcher must justify and negotiate this interpretation, both to research participants as well as to the research community. In this case, observations were shared with the class teachers, both at the time and at the termly meetings, though they were not always clarified with the children. In this sense children were at first more objects than subjects or participants of the research.

Nevertheless, an interesting evolution that occurred as the project progressed was that children moved further into 'subjecthood' as the use of the conversations with them increased. At the outset, as discussed, the extent of the participation of the children in the design of the research was less defined. However, this was a learning curve for me as a new researcher and the flexible design meant that I was able to refine the research questions accordingly. Thus, the methods employed shaped the nature of the enquiry and the new more existential research question became:

- What does participation mean in a reception class?

This question at once moved the interpretation of participation into the children's arena and thus increased the importance of the methods used to elicit communication with them. Denscombe (1998) neatly identifies the way in which interviewees may both inadvertently please and fob off the interviewer. Certainly, both of those features are exacerbated by the inclusion of children in research. Once again assent was compromised by a blurring between the categories of conversation and interview which occurred as a result of the naturalness of the encounter. Denscombe is clear that the difference between conversation and interview should be acknowledged and much of his argument adheres to the 'on the record' (1998, p.110) nature of the latter. In this respect the presence of a tape recorder allowed for the definition of interview to be made clear to the children and to give them a choice in putting their comments on record.

However, the most significant barrier to gaining children's views, in my opinion, was the context for the interviews which, through the very naturalness of the setting, meant that they were answering questions posed by an adult in an adult environment. As Denscombe (1998) points out, it is not the identity of the interviewer that affects the data so much as what the researcher's identity means to the person being interviewed. To deal with this, solutions were attempted in the form of enabling children to operate the tape recorder and ask each other questions; in other words, allowing them to become interviewers as well as interviewees. In this way, the method was again challenged by the theme of the research and I, as researcher, tried to respond to the contradictions and change the children's role within the research.

Whether children appear to speak for themselves or not, Denscombe (1998, p.127) suggests that it is still the researcher's task to 'read between the lines'. Working with children can mean that the medium of interview language is itself inhibiting. It is therefore possible to justify the researcher as narrator on behalf of 'the excluded voice' (Booth and Booth, 1996, p.55). Although applied to research with people who have learning difficulties, this approach can also be usefully considered in relation to research with young children. It involves the researcher coping with and interpreting a level of inarticulateness, unresponsiveness and difficulty with abstract concepts on the part of the subject.

Importantly, in terms of methodology, Booth and Booth (1996) suggest that it is 'the limitations of *our* [my italics] methods' rather than inarticulateness itself that poses problems for the researcher. As they point out, 'even single words can leave a big wash' (p.66) and being 'more attentive to what goes unsaid' (p.63) can provide a more creative approach to interviewing subjects. What they seem to indicate is an extension to the idea of dialogue, in which each word is foregrounded along with its reciprocal silence. This suggests an entirely unconventional poetic of research which infuses the field with highly aesthetic considerations. This means that the researcher as creative interpreter can be viewed in an emancipatory role, particularly when working with less linguistically articulate subjects. In this way, by recording extracts of conversation, my aim was to build a collage of opinion to represent the significance of children's views rather than as a 'database' for computing theory.

However, although children's views became central to the research, it was nevertheless true that the role of the adults was more carefully negotiated than that of the children. The participant teachers and I met together at the end of every term. This meeting was not tape recorded as I was wary of the potentially inhibiting effect of this on the collaborative process of action research. Instead of this, the views of the teachers were recorded through writing in response to some questions. I hesitate to call this a questionnaire in the sense that it was not used, as questionnaires often are, to deal with information from a large number of people. Rather it was used to enable the teachers to write reflectively about the experience of the research process. It was also designed to allow their own questions to be posed; to become the questioner as well as the questioned. In this way they were invited to make their own interpretations to feed directly into the documentation of the research and, more importantly, its analysis and representation.

In summary, the usual techniques for recording evidence from the ethnographic field were utilised, in the form of observation, interview and documentation. However, as the research became more participatory, with regard to the children involved, it became necessary to extend these methods, through the research activities, to less language-based methods which enabled children to contribute, and indeed participate, more fully. These methods, therefore, not only extended the methodology of the research but simultaneously developed a communicative meaning to the research theme.

As specified, the methods used to carry out the research also included a focus on a child in each class who was considered by their parents and teachers to be struggling to settle in. This approach was taken to provide continuity to the observations and throw the concept of belonging into sharp relief. The focus children and a more detailed discussion of the teachers' strengths are included in chapter four. The next section outlines the techniques which were used with groups of the children to allow their expression, as well as a mutual understanding with adults, to develop. These included a variety of forms and activities which aimed to support and provide a context for their language skill.

Participatory techniques with children

O'Kane (2000) points out that the use of specific research methods or techniques with children in participatory research goes beyond their application in a mechanical sense. The success of such techniques lies, instead, in the process of their use in terms of stimulating 'dialogue, reflection and action' (p.138). Indeed such methods form part of a participatory methodology. By using such techniques, in the form of activities with children, the role of the researcher as well as the relationship with the researched becomes more defined and thus more transparent (O'Kane, 2000). This approach originated in work carried out in the context of rural development work, a major influence being the participatory research with illiterate peasants in Latin America of Freire (1972). Thus, this approach is known by the term 'participatory rural appraisal' (PRA). It translates well to use with children because it seeks to reduce reliance on verbal and written forms of communication whilst still allowing for children's own interpretations of 'the relationships, messages and negotiations that structure their lives' (O'Kane, 2000, p.141).

The research project also drew heavily on the mosaic approach which is referred to in chapter four (Clark and Moss, 2001). Devised for use by practitioners as well as researchers, the mosaic approach aims to offer ways of listening to and consulting with young children which are fully inclusive of children with a range of ability. It encompasses a variety of methods which provide an alternative means of expression to language whilst also supporting its use. These methods, like the PRA techniques, include both visual media and the active representation of ideas. Thus photographs, games, tours and mapping are involved, as well as observations and child conferencing. In the project, I drew on a range of visual, symbolic and narrative techniques with children, in order to enable their perspective and expression. A full list of the games and techniques which were used are described in chapters five to eight and summarised in chapter nine. However, an outline of the rationale and design of the activities is included here.

In terms of visual media, the children were able to record their perspective of school by taking digital **photographs** and later identifying and reflecting on them. Prosser (1998, p.19) says that visual anthropology of this kind is 'an exploration by the visual, through the visual, of human sociality'. This includes objects, bodies and thought and constitutes another avenue for critique and reflection to support the interpretive methodology. Photos provide a way to freeze the incessant movement of the classroom and provide a focus for our private interpretations to be discussed and broadened. They also allow children to enter into the practice of observation which penetrates early years practice. It was important that the photos remained the property of the children which they could retain to take home with them.

Ennison and Smith (2000) are at pains to point out that photographs should not be understood as data itself but should be seen only to preserve, store or represent information. They are purely 'signs which bear an iconic resemblance to the reality they represent' (p.3). Interestingly, Ennison and Smith also point to a relationship between Foucault's explication of the panopticon (1979) and the gaze inherent in photographs. This links photographs to practices of power and social control. Therefore the emphasis in the research project was on children's own re-readings of their photos, serving to consolidate, rather than erode, their ownership of the image and their role as research participants. As Ennison and Smith say, the images 'serve as tools for the investigation of concepts and processes' (2000, p.105) and the children operate them.

In terms of action, the project included a variety of games which were either adapted or designed to facilitate and encourage the skills and attitudes needed to support co-operation in the classroom context. However, the richest research techniques used with children drew on symbolic representation of their points of view. These involved using stickers to record perspectives on the decision-makers in their lives and also using tokens to vote with.

The first activity, called 'Who Chooses' evolved from the 'decision-making pocket chart' and a 'pots and beans activity' devised by O'Kane (2000). I adapted this idea for a younger age range and worked with the children in groups of four asking them a set of six questions about decision-making in the course of their day. The children were given a sheet with three shapes symbolising different 'actors' in their lives and were asked to place a sticker in the appropriate shape in a response to each question. This allowed the children to decide on the way to interpret the activity, as well as to gain support and ideas from each other in the process.

The **voting** technique used drew on work done in the field of global education (Fountain, 1990). Fountain suggests that children should each be given a small box that they can make into an individualised 3D voting token. The teachers in this project also devised tokens that would be individual to children in the class so that they could cast their vote in an actual sense without needing to cope with the demands of recording their decisions. Trials suggested that raising hands to indicate a choice led to confusion and some children being unable to inhibit the temptation to raise their hand for every choice available. However the use of a token reinforces the necessity for only one decision to be reached. De Vries and Zan (1994) contrast the methods of polling children and casting ballots, pointing out that polling children can create undue peer group pressure on decision-making. They suggest that casting secret ballots that are unidentifiable might create a different result. In this case, children did make public choices, since the systems were consciously used in order to encourage peer discussion and consensus. This exposure was seen as a positive aspect, with the aim that voting might be a way to engage children to consider the outcomes and process of collective decision-making.

As well as the use of symbols in the activities described above, the use of **narrative** techniques developed from reading stories to the children that dealt with issues of conflict and co-operation. It was apparent that the language of narrative fiction enabled and supported the problem-solving and imaginative skills that children needed to consider other points of view. In contrast, less 'embedded' discussions about participation, even within a small group situation, were soon exhausted. Barone (1995) notes that the story provides 'a format that invites the reader to join in solving a human problem' (p.66) and that this ordering feature of narrative is powerful in allowing the reader to distance herself enough from the present to be able to comment on it. As Barone says, a persuasive educational story is one which lures the readers into 'reconstructing the selves of school people' (p.66). This suggests that stories can act in an emancipatory sense to enable children to rethink outcomes to familiar situations. Thus, they can enter into the narrative and engage with the author with the 'freedom to interpret and evaluate the text from their unique vantage point' (Barone, 1995, p.67).

With this in mind, as the project unfolded, I decided to write a story designed for the purposes of this research, called *Playing Together* about two children who were struggling to agree on what and how to play. At three set points within the story the listeners were invited to offer their solutions to the arguments between the children. This technique aimed to draw on the narrative power of the text and encourage the children to comment on its dilemmas, thereby applying the idea of conflict resolution to themselves 'in real time'. By so doing, I aimed to become an 'artful writer persuader' (Barone, 1995, p.67), allowing children to position themselves as interpreters of fiction. Arguably, it would also be possible to characterise this use of story as emancipatory, in its portrayal of children (imaginary) who sort out their own situation by seeking the help of other children (real) to do so. In this way the story questions the need for adults to be the arbiters of fairness, especially as no one 'is sole proprietor of her or his own story' (Barone, 1995, p.16).

These three participatory methods incorporating visual, symbolic and narrative strategies comprised an essential part of the broader methodological aims for this research. Alderson (2000, p.254) says that a key question in research about children is how adults 'can get beyond the power constraints and expose the intricacies of power in relations between adults and children'. She suggests that it is research *by* children that can achieve this within a context of research about children. Certainly in Hart's (1992) 'Ladder of participation', Alderson's approach to research would achieve a high level. However, it is also the way that methods are used to redistribute communicative power which is crucial to research which involves young children. The techniques described above allowed children to co-determine the course of the project and enabled the adult researchers to listen to a voice other than the echo of their own. They formed not only techniques for involving the children as research participants, but also 'pilot' activities to induct the children into the participatory projects which the participant teachers planned for the third term of the project.

Summary

This chapter has laid out the aims, questions, approach and ethos of the research, as well as the methods and techniques through which it hoped to achieve its aims. The importance of the interdependence of theory and practice has been restated, both in terms of the researcher's own practice and position as well as the methodology which was employed. The schools and teachers in the project have also been introduced.

The subject of the research has been framed as political in form and content which meant that collaboration with class teachers became intrinsic to the research design. The methodology of action research has been defined as a critical theory which focuses on the social and frames truth and action as dynamically interdependent. However, ethnography has also been argued as an important methodology for the study. Its lens of postmodernity and feminism, as developed by Denzin (1997), was viewed as helpful to the researcher's position, both as support to the class teacher in the action research process and as final author of the research account. Ethnography has, therefore, allowed the researcher to become more self-critical and reflexive in the representation of the research participants, particularly those of young children whose voices are rarely heard.

Finally, the research methods have been outlined and their limitations for eliciting communication, particularly with children, have been alluded to. Techniques and activities to improve this communication have been described, drawing on the work developed by O'Kane (2000), using participatory rural appraisal techniques. Subsequently, the rationale and use of visual, symbolic and narrative approaches for developing the research techniques has been outlined.

The next chapter now explores the concept of belonging in greater detail and expands on its links with notions of participation and democracy, whilst also locating key arguments within the context of debates about pedagogy and early childhood education.

Chapter 2

What does it mean to belong?

Belonging in English education

Belonging is a word with multiple resonances which go to the heart of what it means to be human. It suggests deep emotion and is often discussed in the context of religious belief and need fulfilment, crossing discourses of theology and psychology, as well as the fields of sociology and politics which are prioritised in the educational context discussed here. It is also difficult to talk about belonging without also discussing exclusion, since communities exist by virtue of criteria for their membership. There may be contradictory situations where an individual feels that they belong to a community, whilst at the same time being excluded by the criteria of others. Thus, forms of discrimination exist to police the borders of belonging.

In this light, growing attention is being focused by scholars on what a sense of belonging might mean for the study of childhood in a postcolonial world (Cannella and Viruru, 2004; Viruru, 2007). Viruru (2007) suggests that the aggressiveness with which children are targeted as consumers forms a new type of modern imperialism which restructures the social worlds of children, subjecting them to intense advertising and splintering the idea of childhood. Viruru (2007) also points out that children are particularly vulnerable to this new type of imperialism because the sense of belonging, which might provide some defence to this assault, has been tied to a vision of the future associated with modernist ways of thinking. These have then been superseded by new forms of modernity and the idea that the future should not burden the present. Thus, to study childhood from a postcolonial perspective offers a new way of characterising resistance that upholds ideas of ambivalence and evasiveness as the antidote to the ideal of rationalism and new forms of colonisation. These forms of resistance then constitute a way to reconstruct belonging in the postcolonial world.

In terms of English education, a sense of belonging is recognised as important and has found expression in the comparatively recent inclusion of citizenship education in the National Curriculum. The RE curriculum for key stage one (PCA, 2004) likewise asserts the importance of belonging and relates it to 'questions of identity' (p.11). In conjunction with these curriculum documents relating to older children, the *Birth to Three Matters* (DfES, 2002) guidance, which has recently been superseded by the *Statutory Framework for the Early Years Foundation Stage* (DCSF, 2007), also places a sense of belonging as part of a 'strong child' outcome. Thus, the rhetoric of belonging lies firmly at the roots of the current vision for the early childhood curriculum as well as for English education in general. This chapter, therefore, aims to explore how this rhetoric plays out in policy and practice in English early childhood education and care and to examine how this concept is associated with the concept of participation which informed the research project described in this book.

My own interest in the theme of belonging in early years classrooms started with work in the area of disability and inclusion. It seemed to me, and indeed has been well documented by Booth (2000), that the difficulty of converting the theory of inclusion into practice lay in the narrowness of its application in policy terms. Rather than informing, or even transforming, general education policy, the concept of inclusion was being applied to the few (disabled children) rather than the many (children). My view was that this ineffectiveness centred on a misappropriation of the term 'inclusion'. Indeed, Priestley (1999, p.195) says that rather than choosing 'a new name' in the guise of inclusion, disability should be placed at the centre and have meaning reassigned to it. This is, roughly speaking, the ground taken by the social model of disability (Oliver, 1996). Thus, in the context of disability, the project of inclusivity has foundered on its need for a meaning based on theoretical models which signal new, rather than recycled, approaches to our thinking.

Priestley (1999) also suggests that, for the meaning of inclusion to move forward, a challenge is needed to a generalised preoccupation with conceptual dichotomies, identified as 'the logic of identity' (p.102). In place of this process of categorisation, identity should be viewed as an inherently diverse concept which informs inclusion and favours participant action. In this paradigm, identity is constantly under co-construction alongside other identities, which means that the culture of dependency which exists and keeps reinventing itself for disabled children is banished. With this in mind, it seemed that, for my interest in inclusion to be developed and my frustration with its misappropriation to be overcome, it was necessary for the project to characterise inclusion as participation and thereby consider all the children as a group in the classroom context, rather than viewing some children as decontextualised individuals.

This was the perspective which informed my research project and led me into an examination of the arguably equally ambiguous concept of participation. However, in my view the concept of participation has an advantage over the concept of inclusion in education because it has a more direct link with the language of political theory and, in particular, theories of democracy, which are discussed later in this chapter. For this reason, I think it is important for a sense of belonging at the start of school to be characterised as the opportunity to participate, in a political sense, in classroom life and it is the task of this book to examine what a 'political sense' might look like to four- and five-year-old children. If belonging becomes participation, it can be discussed as an overtly political concept and at the same time transform the meaning of that concept. This means that the power to affect and control children, which a sense of belonging suggests, can be debated within a frame of political literacy, rather than the frame of religious belief which is suggested by the RE curriculum.

Arguments about political literacy in the English school curriculum are at the heart of what is known as citizenship education, which has become increasingly relevant to education debates in recent years. In 1998, the 'Crick Report', *Education for Citizenship and the Teaching of Democracy in Schools* (QCA, 1998), was presented to the Secretary of State for Education and Employment with recommendations for the introduction of citizenship education. However, Osler (2000, p.7) argues that the concept of 'political literacy' in this report failed to acknowledge multiple or hybrid identities and therefore did not match an agenda for pupil participation. Furthermore, despite a plural society, the report presents notions of neighbourhood and community affairs as unproblematic whilst, in the same breath, lamenting the levels of apathy, ignorance and cynicism about political and public life (QCA, 1998). The contradictions here are immense.

Nevertheless, a framework for Personal, Social and Health Education and Citizenship (PSHE and C) was introduced into primary schools in September 2000 and schemes of work for key stages one to four followed (QCA, 2002). More recent information on the DfES standards website (last accessed July 2006) includes citizenship in the foundation stage, making reference to links between citizenship activities and 'building' on the early learning goals. There is emphasis on informal aspects of school life, such as playtime, as opportunities to develop active citizenship. In this way the citizenship in the early years of school focuses on the areas of social, personal and communication skills and aims to be cross-curricular in its nature. However, despite this broadening of the notion of citizenship education, there is a danger that the difficult political issues to do with identity, which Osler (2000) raises, and which are central to children's sense of belonging and participation in school, are not being addressed within a citizenship curriculum. With this in mind, the next section delves further into some theoretical interpretations of what a participatory pedagogy in early education might mean.

Critical pedagogy in the early years

In the field of critical pedagogy, Bernstein (1996) implies that participation is a pivotal concept in forging new and different power relations within pedagogical discourse. However, he also points out that the rules which distribute power ensure that any control over alternative possibilities is always tightly regulated. These rules trace back to religious systems in the medieval period which formed the first 'institutionalization of knowledge' (p.45) and they are now more and more controlled by the state. This phenomenon has been made especially clear in recent years in England, with the growth of legislation concerning the early years curriculum.

It may seem a dismal view, yet the concept of participation is central to the possibility of change. This not only offers a way out of pedagogy replicating the values of a society, but it also opens up comparison with a poststructuralist perspective of the same themes. Working with this framework, Walkerdine's (1988) critical exploration of the practices of reason in early education talks about the classroom 'as a place where teacher and child are produced as signs' (p.202). This, as in Bernstein's (1996) analysis, implies deep levels of state control over the educational arena along with attempts in the field of psychology to create a rigid and rationally controlled universe. Thus, it is the practices of these areas of knowledge that produce the terminology of pedagogy and 'what it means to be a subject, to be subjected, within these practices' (p.203). In this way, Walkerdine draws less on the social reproduction approach of Bernstein and more on the poststructural analysis of semiotics which implies disquiet with theoretical schemes which discover how 'truth' is constructed.

Walkerdine (1988) operates with reference to Foucault's (1972) concept of 'veridicality' or the creation of truth. This means that discourses create their own objects, which then become true, and is part of the power of a sign system like language. In Walkerdine's analysis, this concept, as translated into educational practice, means that 'the truth of children is produced in classrooms' (p.204). This in turn creates a 'biologized environment' (p.205) in which the idea of a normally developing child and its reverse are imbued with significance. Similarly, the power of the teacher comprises management of the classroom and knowledge itself, corresponding to Foucault's notion of 'discipline'. In this notion, the discourse of reason obscures and denies power relations such that mastery of rational argument becomes an effective means of regulation.

Thus, so-called 'child-centred' education, which is synonymous with the early years, begins to take on a sinister meaning, based on its double denial of the theoretical issues at stake. It opens the way for a tighter degree of regulation and observation, with paradoxically less opportunity for deviation from an imaginary norm. In this vision of the natural child, the indisputable truth which it constructs provides us with a representation of the power which regulates citizens in the democratic order. The implication is that reason becomes an automatic feature of child development, giving us the basis for a government which 'covers over both its sociality and the unconscious lurking beneath' (Walkerdine, 1988, p.5).

Child-centred education, therefore, runs the risk of basing pedagogy on a latent assumption that consciousness exists independent of the discourse which constructs it. Usher and Edwards (1994) suggest that it is an effect of power that a person is seen as a foundation who has interests, rather than as affected by that power. Subjectivity does not pre-exist power and in this way learners are inscribed with dispositions to learn. The irony is that identity in a child-centred pedagogy is usually seen as primarily asocial, whilst in fact, in Foucault's view, identity is deeply social and created by power because 'society without power relations can only be an abstraction' (1982, p.222).

This view can also be supported by perspectives emanating from poststructural thinkers in the field of psychology. Lacan (1977) positions the subject as intrinsically social, formed by a desire for the recognition of others and therefore constituted by this recognition. Thus, self-consciousness follows a socially constructed consciousness and defies biological determination. Importantly, language and the unconscious are the elements through which meanings are constantly made and lost, one consistently toppling the other with desire, as the thread which tries unsuccessfully to bind them together and close the gap. This means that communication is fundamental to a sense of selfhood: 'What constitutes me as subject is my question' (Lacan, 1977, p.86). In pedagogical terms this means that knowledge becomes discontinuous and, as Walkerdine (1988) suggests, does not move in a linear fashion towards uncomplicated mastery. Instead there are 'diversions and sudden breakthroughs' (Usher and Edwards, 1994, p.79). This is the unconscious in action, and centred in a child it makes child-centred education far from the liberal concept it appears to be.

Thus, Walkerdine (1988) finds that the talk of children does not match the abstracted idea of reason but is invested in 'the pleasure of beating and the pain of being beaten' (p.201). This demonstrates the importance of her analysis in the interpretation of empirical research. Her critique, which bears comparison with Bernstein's, but also, as stated, relies on Foucauldian insights, enables a view of pedagogy in which nothing is certain. This is important because the implication is that challenging the claim to know becomes central to resistance (Walkerdine, 1988). This means that, for a participatory pedagogy to penetrate the early years classroom, it must encompass the construction of knowledge itself. Although Foucault would hardly endorse a leap to such conclusions, it would be consistent with Lacan's ideas to suggest that participation allows for the repressed unconscious to articulate itself and therefore for the teacher to position oneself as a co-learner in the task of constructing knowledge. As Stanton (1983, p.88) points out in a discussion of Lacan's work:

> the pupils then would be allowed to extend their analysis to their environment. To create the space they live in rather than just fit in with the set rules. Literally. To paint. To build. To co-operate. To participate. The limit then would be the analysis of the transference.

Critical pedagogy is a diverse field. By starting with Bernstein and following with Walkerdine and the postmodernist thinkers she refers to, it is possible to

see the move in criticism from all-embracing 'grand' narratives to the inde-
terminate number of micro-strands which attention to language demands.
Usher and Edwards (1994) state that 'critical pedagogy is a powerful and
attractive narrative of education which both takes account of and challenges
aspects of the postmodern moment' (p.216). Thus the demands of action and
change do not sit easily alongside the ironic language games which a poststructural analysis can lead to. However, since the role of language is so
crucial to teaching, particularly if we extend language to cover other forms of
symbolic communication, I would argue that it is important to retain a poststructural lens on pedagogy.

This diverse view of critical pedagogy also takes into account the pitfalls
and mistakes inherent in attempting to communicate with others who are
distanced by age and power relations. The implication of this is that participation must be central to teaching and learning in an era when identity itself
has become so elusive. However, the process of participation itself is also
opaque. As Usher and Edwards (1994) point out, 'subjects can only understand themselves and the world of "things" through their immersion and
participation in the world of signs' (p.208). Arguably, therefore, education
must provide the space for signs themselves to be democratised if political
participation is to mean anything. In this way, I would argue that the politics
of language are indeed intrinsic to pedagogy and, therefore, in the broader
guise of 'communication', will inform this study.

The problem with 'participation'

Despite the possibility discussed above, namely that addressing participation
might provide a challenge to education, the concept, like that of inclusion,
has been absorbed into dominant discourses in education that always seek
new ways to govern. Dahlberg and Moss (2005) cite Foucault (1980) to suggest that these discourses are 'regimes of truth' that make 'assumptions and
values invisible' (p.142). Thus, participation as a practice struggles to hang
onto its democratic roots because of its attractiveness within a consumer culture as a tool for making people feel consulted. This process of fake
consultation sidesteps any struggle for mutual understanding and means that
behaviour can be directed and controlled.

In educational work, this has resulted in the occurrence of the participation
'manual'. These are often produced by children's organisations and local councils and they provide examples of consultation with children. There is an
appeal to individuality which at the same time homogenises groups of children into the appearance of a single voice. Young children may be in the
process of developing the executive skills which allow for more adult ways of
collective consultation in the form of debate. However, this process of development is implicitly viewed as a reason to preclude efforts to encourage
mutual recognition of each other's rights'. This means that the dominance of

the 'individualistic gaze' (Fulcher, 1989, p.263), that isolates children with disabilities, requires that children are consulted and make choices as consumers, with little regard for each other as rights' holders. This then hijacks the democratic and political meaning of participation as a process that involves collective, as well as individual, decision-making.

Typical examples of the trend to consult children in this way are projects focusing on environments which have been carried out, often in areas of social deprivation. One example of this is the 'London on your doorstep' project in which young children's perspectives on their surroundings were recorded using 'easy and reliable methods' (Emerson, 2001, p.8). Children's views were collected: photographs taken, comments made and pictures drawn. A community artist was then involved in working with the children on a mural depicting their ideal environment. Whilst this type of project certainly involves children in a meaningful and socially worthwhile activity, it nevertheless does not address the possibility that children may hold opposing views which may be equally valid. The difficult part, therefore, of a consultation of this kind is not so much the adults listening to the children as the children listening to each other and developing their views collectively prior to these being recorded as 'the child's perspective'. For this to happen, adults may need to be involved to provide a framework for a process that is probably very far from the 'easy' it suggests. This is one example of many such potentially worthwhile social projects which tend to portray the process of children's participation without the suggestion of disagreement or complexity.

This potential undermining of the concept of participation reflects some of the debates about the nature of democracy itself. It is therefore important to understand these debates, particularly as they are reflected in the anxieties which children starting school are vulnerable to. In the light of these debates, it will then be possible to begin to characterise what makes participation distinct as a valid form of democracy, rather than what makes it false.

Theories of democracy

The tendency in what I call the participation 'manuals' to deal with consultation but not fairness and collectivity can be tied in with key debates by theorists who view democracy as the politics of either 'recognition' or 'redistribution'.

The controversy about emphasising features of recognition and identity in discourses of democracy centres on whether this approach can address fundamental material issues of inequality if it concerns itself primarily with difference in terms of identity. Fraser (1995) refers to this split in models of democracy as a transition from the idea of social democracy as the equal distribution of resources to the idea of social justice as 'the recognition of the personal dignity of all individuals' (Honneth, 2002, p.43). Honneth (2002), however, finds the division which Fraser outlines to be false. He uses Hegelian philosophy to demonstrate that concepts of self-awareness and the moral progress of a society are linked by the mediation of 'intersubjective struggles' which mean that social boundaries must be widened in order for resolution to take place (p.41). He views the politics of recognition not as disillusionment but as 'an increase in moral sensibility' (p.42). Furthermore, he finds that identity politics are not new and do not challenge either material interests or legal concerns. Indeed, struggles over distribution are themselves 'locked into a struggle for recognition' as they are symbolic of the socio–cultural ordering of the value of different activities (p.54). In other words, Honneth suggests, material goods are awarded to different members of a society based on principles of recognition.

Although Honneth's (2002) notion of recognition, as detailed above, may differ from Fraser's more individualistic notion, nevertheless this can be viewed as a unifying argument as regards different understandings of democracy. It also includes the conclusion that unemployment means that many people are denied the experience of gaining a sense of value and social esteem through their contribution to social production. In Honneth's view, this means that struggles for recognition will grow and be directed at the institutionalised nature of the symbolic and material recognition that different activities and abilities accrue (p.54).

Bauman (2002), however, identifies more significant risks and less inherent good in recognition per se than Honneth. He finds that it is often 'negative' and detached from its seekers unless it is positively aligned with social justice. Negative recognition is endemic of 'the relativist precipice' (p.145) that we live on where difference 'may have to be paid for with distributive handicap in the competitive game of resources and rewards' (p.144). However, Bauman also realises that the politics of recognition are an unavoidable symptom of the times we live in and he cites Rorty's (1998) analysis of the move from 'movement' to 'campaign' politics as the way forward (p.146). Ultimately, it seems that campaign politics is the strategy which links distributive justice and a policy of recognition and gives social justice its meaning (p.147), since on its own, recognition falls into an ineffective and therefore dangerous pit. In essence then, self-realisation does not imply the fairness of redistribution which Honneth draws from philosophy; for Bauman, politics is a more conscious historical act. This suggests that, when consulted, children need to experience real, rather than token, power. It also suggests that participation with children in school should incur an educational dimension in order to develop collective and social responsibility.

Both Honneth's and Bauman's accounts of contemporary democracy agree that participation and the experience of co-operation are the way that an individual gains a sense of recognition and integration within society. However, the mechanisms through which minority groups might be heard and gain representation in the present liberal democratic political system are not explored. Phillips (1993) feels that the way to greater fairness for minority groups is through increasing procedures for group consultations (p.97) rather than a requirement for quotas of representatives. She says that even oppressed groups have within them a diversity of individual concerns and perspectives which may be best developed within a liberal democratic model, whereas a politics of difference might advocate a type of group representation which constrains, and maybe even stereotypes, the views of its members. Bauman (2002) suggests that, whatever the system, it is important that voicing opinions and concerns attaches to material and social outcomes. In relation to research with children, who can be seen as representative of a minority group, the social and material outcome of participation can also serve as motivation to participate further.

Young (2000) has developed the issue of minority group representation debated by Phillips and has also tried to schematise the link between concepts of inclusion and democracy. This is achieved by exploring what is called a 'deliberative model of democracy' and making it a means of 'collective problem-solving' (p.6). The authority of this depends on the diverse opinions of all the members of a society and it expands the boundaries of a narrow deliberative style to include 'greeting, rhetoric and narrative' (p.7) as styles of communication which include a wider cultural brief. Young is concerned with a theory of communicative democracy which is both practical and critical of the shortcomings of most political processes. This makes it intrinsically educational in its aim to encompass a range of perspectives and correct the bias of a partial perspective (p.83). The conditions for this inclusive form of democracy are that participants are attentive to one another and must therefore justify their claims in ways that are acceptable to all. It means that different groups can voice their interests 'in ways that meet conditions of reasonableness and publicity' (p.119).

Young (2000) is also critical of Habermas's (1984, 1987) theory of communicative action which suggests that the use of rhetoric is manipulation which serves the speaker's own ends. Young's view of rhetoric is more positive and she sees it as instrumental in furthering political communication and enabling participants to solve collective problems (p.66). She advocates rhetoric as fostering inclusion on the basis that people are often excluded precisely because of their *way* of expressing themselves rather than because of *what* they say. Thus, she concludes that, to be inclusive, people must be listened to, unless they are completely disrespectful of others. We should also notice how some people in political conflicts are dismissed because of their style (p.70). In this respect, Young echoes Butler (1997) who feels that Habermasian concepts, such as 'consensus' and 'norm', only define themselves in relation to exclusions. The 'necessarily difficult task' (p.91) of forging real consensus can only come from various locations of culture. Butler, therefore, like Young, contests and arguably extends Habermas's notion of the ideal speech situation in order to encompass the concept of diverse culture, difference and change.

Clearly all the political theorists referred to in this section agree that a democracy that involves political equality is more complex than having the right to vote and they all envisage struggle of some kind to achieve it. For Phillips (1993) and Young (2000) this relies on improved systems of communication within the wider democratic political system. From their viewpoint as women, they know that this is not a neutral process. However, they advocate that systems can, nevertheless, adopt rules and procedures that allow for as many people as possible to influence them. The connections here with educational theory are evident and it is therefore unsurprising to find that many educationalists have linked together concepts of democracy with a vision for education and theories of learning.

By outlining key theories of democracy, it becomes possible to understand how educational institutions as well as educationalists are affected by political philosophy and exemplify it within their own systems and organisations. With regard to an ethos of participation, these institutions face the problems expressed in the critical pedagogy of Bernstein: of whether they can overcome the inclination to reproduce capitalist tendencies to 'consumerise' and bury participation within existing bureaucratic systems, or whether they can find a way for participatory practices to affect and change these systems. It is thus to the study of educational systems that we look to next.

Democracy, participation and education

Michael Apple is one of the educational theorists who link together theories of democracy with education. He suggests that schools (and indeed other educational institutions) are particularly interesting as they embody and exemplify ideology (1982). Apple (1982, p.171) goes on to identify capitalism, rather than liberalism, as that which really undermines the substance of democracy 'in its quest for efficiency, expert authority, rationalisation, and increased discipline'. This contrasts not only with the essentially classical conception of democracy as a moral ideal but also with the greater individualism of liberal democracy, which in the British tradition can be traced back to the influence of J.S. Mill. As Apple says: 'In a time when capital and the state... can no longer "afford" substantive democracy, we need to reappropriate democracy as a discourse and a set of practices back from the right' (p.172).

Nixon et al. (1996) tie the nature of learning to the nature of democracy thereby allowing education to illuminate the impact of social classification. In this vision of a learning society concepts of communication and participation are combined and 'the central task of the learning school is the reconstruction of agency' (p.117). Change may not be dramatic but seeds are sown for democratic change. The key to this process of enlightenment has to be the motivation to learn and this view prioritises the position of the teacher. Motivation is nurtured by valuing and encouraging students and implies that cultural diversity encompasses both the curriculum and teaching resources. Nixon et al. (1996)

place recognition and reaffirmation of difference at the heart of their view of a democratic and learner-centred education system. In this way they envisage 'the necessary cultural renewal of active citizenship' (p.124) and can be seen to share Young's model of deliberative democracy (2000).

Nixon *et al.* (1996) state that it is the essentially creative contribution which learners make to a society which then challenges assumptions that are made about the identities of its members. They also say that debate should not be confined to school but involve consultation on a wider scale so that motivation and purpose are brought into classrooms, as well as moving outwards from them through an education that assumes active citizenship. It is therefore clear that many educationalists feel that education can play a part in transforming the dominant model of democracy which identifies with the interest of capital and a consumer-driven society. This vision, which thrives on the principles of a participatory model of democracy, is driven by a belief in the capacity of education to influence and benefit from the socio-political trend towards the concept of a learning society.

However, in contrast to this vision of a learning society, the bureaucratic effect of the current capitalist, sometimes called 'contemporary', model of democracy leads to a huge amount of organisational pressure on institutions such as schools. Skrtic (1991, p.177) throws some light on this barrier through an analysis of professional bureaucracy as a 'performance' rather than a 'problem-solving' organisation which is premised on the 'principle of standardisation' (p.182). Skrtic points out that there is a contradiction between the substantive rationality of democracy and the formal rationality of the bureaucracy which it needs for administration. Because of this, the dynamism of democracy is restrained by the resistance to change of bureaucracy. Problematically, this suggests that inclusive participation as a democratic ideal cannot satisfy a transformative agenda within a predominantly bureaucratic school system. The solution, according to Skrtic (1991), is to reconfigure schools as 'adhocratic' (p.184) rather than bureaucratic organisations. This fits neatly with a participatory ideal in its absence of hierarchy and open-ended structure.

Summary

This chapter has explored the need to interrogate meanings of key concepts such as belonging, inclusion and participation, both before and concurrently with attempts to accommodate them in education. The relationship of these concepts with critical pedagogy and ideas of democracy is an important one which needs grasping, so that they do not become part of the dominant discourses in our society, which fail to challenge existing practices and motivate change (Dahlberg and Moss, 2005).

Educational thinkers such as Walkerdine draw on a range of poststructural social theorists to outline a devastating critique of both developmental and child-centred approaches to education. Primarily, therefore, the task of participatory practice is to challenge what counts as knowledge for adults, as well as for children. Furthermore, what counts as participation with children has to address the possibility of conflict and opposing views, rather than viewing children as an homogenous group with one perspective.

Debates about democracy turn on key issues to do with the relative importance of redistribution of resources and the recognition of the members in a society (Honneth, 2002; Bauman, 2002; Young, 2000). A specific problem has been the extent to which capitalist ideas have undermined both liberal and classical notions of democracy (Apple, 1982). All these issues affect education but Nixon *et al.* (1996) suggest that a learning society based on active citizenship is a creative solution to reconnecting democracy, participation and education. Ultimately, however, the problems which education faces in encouraging democratic and participatory practices may have more to do with the growth of educational bureaucracy and its incompatibility with democratic aims (Skrtic, 1991).

The greatest challenge to the bureaucracy of an educational institution must, arguably, be those within it who do not understand and abide by its rules. This includes the youngest children, and therefore early years pedagogies have often contested dominant practices in the organisation of schools and exemplified the 'adhocracy' which Skrtic (1991) suggests challenges bureaucracy. Therefore, we look in the next chapter to policy and practice in early childhood settings, in order to explore how participation and a sense of belonging are characterised there.

Chapter 3

Participation in early childhood education

The early years classroom as a site for participation

Arguably, the early years classroom is in the best position to fit with the adhocratic approach advocated in the last chapter. This is because teaching practices, and indeed policy documents, often stress the importance of flexibility in the organisation of activities; for instance, the *Curriculum Guidance for the Foundation Stage* (DfEE, 2000, p.11) states in its principles that this should include 'provision for the different starting points from which children develop their learning'. It also states that this should be available indoors and outdoors. Furthermore, opportunities need to be available for activities initiated by children themselves as well as adults. More recent documentation, including the *Statutory Framework for the Early Years Foundation Stage* (DCSF, 2007) and the *Key Elements of Effective Practice* (KEEP) (DfES, 2005a), demonstrate overt connection to examples of research such as REPEY (Research into Effective Pedagogy in the Early Years), (Siraj-Blatchford *et al.*, 2002) EPPE (Effective Provision of Pre-school Education) (Sylva *et al.*, 2004) and SPEEL (Study of Pedagogical Effectiveness in Early Learning) (Moyles *et al.*, 2002). Thus, KEEP (p.11), drawing from this research, suggests that one element of effective practice is that 'practitioners need to develop, demonstrate and continuously improve their understanding of the individual and diverse ways that children develop and learn'.

These exhortations to foundation stage practitioners are based on the implicit notion that children are constructors of their own learning. However, it is not clear whether such directives actively promote an adhocratic classroom, or indeed offer any real opportunities for the meta-learning that participation offers. De Vries and Zan (1994), writing about a USA context from a 'constructivist', Piagetian viewpoint, suggest that 'the conditions for sociomoral development are the same conditions for intellectual development' (p.2). Although, like the recent documents cited, they adopt a developmental viewpoint, which is mostly contested in this book, they nevertheless suggest that children can make decisions and vote on classroom matters in a power-sharing manner. This goes beyond any recent foundation stage curriculum advice to English practitioners and forms an essential part of the 'sociomoral' atmosphere in the classroom which, in turn, nurtures children's own sense of social and moral responsibility.

De Vries and Zan implicitly acknowledge that the development of children's empathy is not wholly egocentric. As Pritchard (1996) states, citing educational psychologist William Damon (1990), the practice of sharing begins as soon as children interact with each other (Pritchard, 1996, p.13). This means that concepts such as fairness, equality and merit, in other words the problems of distributive justice, are often being dealt with before children are two years old. Nevertheless, Damon emphasises, it is 'reasoned adult encouragement' (cited in Pritchard, 1996, p.14) that transforms this early moral response, in children around the age of four years old, to a sense of the obligation to share connected to ideas of right and wrong.

De Vries and Zan (1994), however, not only promote an ethos of decision-making as a tool for young children to learn about morality, they also provide a pedagogy which seems to extend beyond their position as developmentalists. Though their democratic brief does not explore principles in great theoretical detail, it does provide a significant amount of practical advice as to how to make participation integral to classroom life. In this respect, it usefully contextualises a developmental approach to young children's moral and intellectual education within a democratic social framework and will be returned to to illuminate the participatory practices discussed in subsequent chapters.

Listening to children and beyond

Despite the arguably half-hearted approach to participation in recent DCSF curriculum documents, in the wider field of early years research in England, participation has been characterised as listening to children and also, less frequently, as addressing issues of inequality. This research recognises that young children's views need to be approached and ascertained through active and multi-sensory methods. At the forefront of this field is the well documented 'mosaic approach', devised and developed by Clark and Moss (2001) at the Thomas Coram Institute in London. The approach is advocated with a variety of purposes, in terms of audit information, special needs reviews and the planning of areas of provision. Most importantly, perhaps, it claims to enable children to become 'co-constructors' (Moss, 1998, p.4) with adults of rules and responsibilities. The multi-method elements of the approach include observation, child-conferencing, photographs, tours and mapping and it aims to be reflexive, routine, adaptable and embedded in practice. Significantly, 'there is no developmental map to follow' (Moss, 1998, p.4).

The strength of the mosaic approach seems to lie in its understated 'everydayness' which is well within the grasp of the youngest children in a nursery setting. In this respect, it does not comprise the extra set of activities that participation often implies for older children in more formal educational circumstances. The mosaic approach also takes the emphasis away from language skills as a sole tool for consultation and enables repeated opportunities for adults to reflect on the messages children are giving them. It does, however, still rely on adults to create a genuine, rather than token, forum for participation. Otherwise, as Moss (2001, p.17) points out, the danger is that 'listening to children can become a subtle but effective way to control them'. The younger the children, the greater risk this must be. Thus, one of the dangers of listening to children is that it will not reflect or inform systemic change. Indeed, in support of this, Sheridan and Pramling Samuelsson's (2001) Swedish study of children's influence on their pre-schools confirms that, although children do often make decisions about their own activities, they rarely influence the overall organisation set by the teachers. Therefore, children's practice of democracy becomes limited to the activities and structures that have already been decided.

A further danger of listening to children, via the mosaic approach, is that whilst it may facilitate the consultative aspect of participation it does not, in itself, help children to make sense of difference. This means that the vital social inclusion issues inherent in participation could be left unchallenged and unaddressed in a blaze of decontextualised 'listening'. This issue has often been ignored by early years practitioners in the belief that young children are oblivious to social difference and inequality. However as Road (2004, p.1) says, young children do form values and responses to differences that they notice in people's outward physical characteristics. This means that early education has to overtly encompass a positive understanding of difference in order to acknowledge the opinion-forming process that young children are subject to, as well as subject of. Jeffcoate (1980) found that, in the classroom, white nursery children appeared not to discriminate between pictures of white and black people in different jobs, yet outside of the classroom, without teacher input, derisory comments were made about the pictures of black people. This case study demonstrates that it is not enough to limit young children's participation to consultation and choice without addressing issues of inequality and difference.

Further developments of work on listening to children led by Dahlberg and Moss (2005) have, however, acknowledged the issue of difference more vigorously. Listening has, thus, been redefined as a concept which incorporates a poststructuralist standpoint. Moss et al. (2005) go as far as to say that listening is 'dangerous' in that there are inherent risks that those listening might believe that they stand outside of power relations. Thus, they advocate that listening should move beyond its current meaning to encompass 'pedagogy and a way of researching life, a culture and an ethic, a continuous process and relationship' (p.13). This approach provides a useful antidote to the possible leanings towards sentimentalism that the pedagogy of listening to children can inspire. However, it also recognises that the concept has enabled early childhood services to become loci of ethical and political practice (Dahlberg and Moss, 2005). It is in this guise that early childhood policy opens itself up to critique and the truly reflexive practices that are needed for practitioners to develop children as future citizens.

Participation in recent early childhood policy

The driving force behind interest in children's participation can be traced to the UN Convention on the Rights of the Child (1989) which paved the way for children's participatory rights to influence worldwide legislation concerning children. This concept has influenced much subsequent legislation and culminated in the governmental creation of a Children's Ministry in 2002 to bring together the delivery of services for children under one unifying umbrella. Alongside these changes, many key pieces of UK legislation relevant to children, such as The Children Act (1989), The SEN and Disability Act (2001) and The Children Act (2004), have sought to include children's decision-making in a legal framework, though often this has been translated in a somewhat tokenistic fashion. As with the UNCRC, there must be doubt about the commitment to genuine consultation with children inherent in these measures. Children are often constructed as victims of injustices in the system but the solution to improvements in this situation rarely involves them in a systematic way. Furthermore, without critical exploration of concepts of childhood, it is difficult to envisage sustained development of the concept of children's rights and its implications beyond a protectionist outlook. Clearly, however, this legislative trend towards at least referring to, if not enabling, children's participation in decision-making has had a growing impact on the content and quantity of policy affecting children's education and care in the past five years.

The most influential policy affecting early years provision in England in recent years has been the *Every Child Matters* programme (DCSF, 1995–2008). This sets out five outcome strands, including one entitled 'Making a Positive Contribution'. This covers themes related to participation and is translated into the five aims (worded as directives) below for children and young people.

1 engage in decision-making and support the community and environment;
2 engage in law-abiding and positive behaviour in and out of school;
3 develop positive relationships and choose not to bully or discriminate;
4 develop self-confidence and successfully deal with significant life changes and challenges;
5 develop enterprising behaviour.

Although this approach to participatory aims attempts to give meaning to structural issues by including reference to relationships and self-confidence, yet there is no mention of equality and only tacit recognition of difference in the reference to discrimination. Furthermore, although the *Every Child Matters* website (DCSF, 1995–2008) does provide links to detailed research into participation (Kirby *et al.,* 2003) it also acknowledges, with regard to involving children and young people in participation, that:

> It is difficult to translate commitment into practice that is meaningful for children and young people, effective in bringing about change and which becomes embedded within the organisational ethos.
>
> (DCSF, 1995–2008)

This acknowledgment of the difficulties inherent in making participation genuine, whilst refreshing in its honesty, may encourage doubt that this work is central to the practitioner role. Therefore, it colludes with the view of participation as peripheral and optional and continues to exclude children and young people from the policy process, which in turn creates a curriculum they are not invited to co-construct.

Participation and an early childhood curriculum

Whilst the *Every Child Matters* programme (DCSF, 1995–2008) attempts to provide guiding principles and a co-ordinating role for social policy concerning children and young people, it is the role of curriculum documentation to spell out what it means in practice for early childhood education and care. The recent *Statutory Framework for the Early Years Foundation Stage* (DCSF, 2007) promotes a developmental view of children's learning which is thorough to the point of leaving very little discretion to practitioners. It has also extended its brief, beyond that of the previous *Curriculum Guidance for the Foundation Stage* (DfEE, 2000), to cover the education and care of children from birth to five years old.

However, despite its extensiveness, the *Statutory Framework for the Early Years Foundation Stage* (DCSF, 2007) provides little motivation for exploring participation as a major part of young children's learning, in the way that Nixon *et al.* (1996) suggest. This may be because the main guidance on participation (Kirby *et al.,* 2003) referred to by the *Every Child Matters* programme (DCSF, 1995–2008) does not specifically focus on young children's participation. This means that participation remains relatively unexplored with regard to the policy that informs early years curriculum development. Thus, although the *Statutory Framework for the Early Years Foundation Stage* (DCSF, 2007) states that 'all children are citizens and have rights and entitlements' and 'all children have an equal right to be listened to and valued in the setting', further support for developing a clear rationale for participatory practice with young children is still needed. Indeed, children's voices are absent from the curriculum document and their perspectives are filtered through developmental norms and a 'manual' approach to supporting activities. An example of this 'manual approach' is contained in *Excellence and Enjoyment: Social and Emotional Aspects of Learning. Getting On and Falling Out: Foundation Stage* (DfES, 2005b). Although the learning outcomes for activities are phrased in children's words (for example, 'I can play with other children'; 'I know how to be friendly'; 'I can say sorry when I have been unkind'), it is unclear whether or how young children themselves were consulted in choosing these outcomes or how these activities link to learning beyond social and emotional contingencies.

In the REPEY study, Siraj-Blatchford *et al.* (2002) confirmed that activities that engendered shared thinking were effective in extending children's thinking. Whilst these type of activities are promoted to some extent by the latest DCSF early years curriculum (2007) through links to research such as REPEY and the idea of 'sustained shared thinking' (DCSF, 2007, p.9), nevertheless, shared thinking as linked to participation is not apparent in the main tenets of the curriculum. It is tempting to wonder if its detailed prescription intrinsically creates a barrier to the development of these kinds of activities. An example of participatory shared thinking is found in the work of Haynes and Murris (2000) who link citizenship and thinking by teaching young children philosophy using a story approach. This introduces the idea of dialogue to children, showing them the process and the pleasure 'of thinking about what things mean' (p.14). Although the approach is language based, it is accessible to very young children by building on what they already know and can do. This is an example of thinking skills being placed in a participatory, rather than narrowly cognitive, context at an early stage in education.

The suggestion that participation should be an integral part of the curriculum informed by an ideal of community life is asserted by Kirby *et al.* (2003). They argue that participation is a 'multi-layered concept' (p.144) which, to be meaningful, must be considered as a process, 'not simply the application of isolated participation activities or events' (p.145). The fact that they find a lack of evidence that children's participation is effective in generating 'substantial' change (p.31) reinforces my assertion that many of the current, well-intentioned, activity-based participation manuals are doomed to failure without precipitant strategic intervention.

For notable examples of participatory work embedded in an early years curriculum we need to look outside of England and the UK. In Italy, the Reggio Emilia charter of rights (Malaguzzi *et al.*, 2005, p.214) claims that 'creative intelligence' is formed 'through an ongoing process of differentiation and integration with other people and other experiences'. This suggests that children's rights are intrinsically inclusive and related to cognition. The Reggio philosophy organises its pre-schools around 'the foundations of educational planning and research' (Malaguzzi *et al.*, 2005, p.29) and thus the design of the environment is based on a system of interconnections and interaction. This interaction includes families, school staff and teachers and it attempts to nurture the professional growth and knowledge of individuals. In this way, the importance of organisation is stated as a dynamic educational tool which also promotes democratic participation and, importantly, they are conceived of as one and the same in a vision of the future of schooling.

The Reggio Emilia approach to early education and care is best known for its pedagogical emphasis on encouraging children to explore and understand experiences through modes of expression that are considered more natural to them. Thus, children can express their ideas through representations such as print, art, construction, drama, music and puppetry. This also fits well with the multi-method mosaic approach which also supports children's language skills through the use of diverse media. The essential principle in these practices is that children are viewed as competent and, indeed, masterful communicators who are also encouraged to collaborate to develop multiple perspectives (OECD, Directorate for Education, 2004).

The *Te Whaariki* early childhood curriculum in New Zealand (NZ Ministry of Education, 1996) also embodies strong ideas about the participation of the community in early childhood education. As discussed in the introduction to the book, it is modelled on a sociocultural approach to childhood which follows the ideas of Bronfenbrenner. According to Smith and May (2006), it makes a political statement about children, their uniqueness, ethnicity and rights in New Zealand society. Influences on a child's learning are portrayed as a set of nested dolls with the inner 'level' consisting of the immediate learning environment. This level includes the concept that individual rights should be met with the development of associated responsibilities. The outer level then incorporates the nation's beliefs and values about children and their care and education, supporting the idea that children's rights do not occur in isolation from the wider structures of society.

In the *Te Whaariki* curriculum (1996) we can once again identify that links are made between children's learning and wellbeing and the participation of community in an early childhood programme. Thus, identity is seen as a social construction. There is strong emphasis throughout on Maori language and culture as representative of the idea of community and, in this way, cultural diversity is recognised. Finally, it is stated that dispositions to 'reason, investigate and collaborate' (p.44) are encouraged by children's immersion in 'communities where people discuss rules, are fair, explore questions about how things work, and help each other' (p.44). In this way, participation is seen as a social aim which includes children in an educational way by developing their ability to learn at the same time as initiating them into community life.

Farquhar (2005) explains how the political intent of *Te Whaariki* was shaped by the goals of the women's movement and the early childhood community. She also suggests that it can be seen 'as a text that has allowed for a plethora of narratives to be inscribed upon it' (p.4). Nevertheless, she also points out that there remains a rift between the goals of *Te Whaariki* and the economic policy climate in which it operates. In the context of an international market-based economy and the need for women in the workforce, the child has become necessarily 'suited to the needs of capitalism' and childcare has replaced the family as the institution which specialises in early childhood. Thus, New Zealand's strategic plan for early childhood aims to get children out of the home because 'families are not well informed about the value of ECE (early childhood education) to their children's development' (NZ Ministry of Education, 2002, p.6). Clearly, this poses contradictions with a curriculum that espouses the importance of a child's sense of belonging and it reinforces that the economic context of curricula that promote participation cannot be ignored.

Despite the inevitable contradictions posed by economic policies and contexts, this book, nevertheless, supports the Reggio Emilia and *Te Whaariki* curriculum approaches. In these approaches, participation builds on positive adult/child relationships and is relevant to personal not just public decisions, as well as being integral to daily practices. However, England has not provided curriculum guidance which promotes participation to a similar extent. Furthermore, legal structures to support pupil participation are often more in evidence in other European countries (Davies and Kirkpatrick, 2000) than anywhere in the UK. In England, it appears that research and academic enquiry, rather than legislation or supporting policy documents, provides the forum for a properly penetrating look at pupil participation. Dahlberg and Moss (2005) are thorough in their theoretical justification for early childhood services as loci of political and ethical practice and the report by Kirby *et al.* (2003) sets the scene for the scale of educational change that is needed for participation to become a reality, not just another example of policy rhetoric. The message is unequivocal: 'meaningful and sustainable participation requires organisations to change' (p.144). Clearly, therefore, research into participation is action research at its most fundamental.

Summary

This chapter contends that an adhocratic approach to the classroom is not sufficiently supported by policy and curriculum documents which relate to young children in England. This is despite evidence that this approach would build a 'sociomoral atmosphere' in the class which would also enhance children's intellectual development (De Vries and Zan, 1994). However, despite the limitations of government guidance in this respect, examples of pioneering participatory pedagogies in early years education in England can be found. These include the mosaic approach (Clark and Moss, 2001) and the development of approaches to listening to children (Dahlberg and Moss, 2005). However, it is important that listening to children is not taken out of a socio-political context. This might exclude the issue of difference explored by Jeffcoate (1980) and undermine the necessary struggle involved in trying to reach agreement in an arena which recognises many possible valid options.

It is, therefore, important that this pedagogical approach invites continual critique of early childhood services and does not fall into a trap of sentimentalism (Dahlberg and Moss, 2005).

The problem in English policy for children and young people, as represented by the *Every Child Matters* programme (DCSF, 1995–2008), is that, although lip service is paid to the participatory practices and outcomes which find their roots in the UNCRC, curriculum documentation for young children, in the form of the *Statutory Framework for the Early Years Foundation Stage* (DCSF, 2007), lacks teeth in this respect. Therefore, it is possible that attempts to tie participation to pedagogic philosophy will result in a fragmented and partial approach, if the importance of a holistic vision is not realised. The primarily developmental approach of the English foundation stage curriculum detracts from wider community issues in which children could play a part. It also precludes children and practitioners from playing a significant role in curriculum development. In contrast, further afield, the pedagogies of Reggio Emilia in Italy (Rinaldi, 2005) and *Te Whaariki* (NZ Ministry of Education, 1996) in New Zealand, trace serious, systemic attempts to place pupil, parent and community participation high on an early childhood agenda. Nevertheless, the extent to which these pedagogies can challenge economic policies which undermine the family has yet to be determined.

In England, it has been argued that, it has been left to research and academic enquiry to explore the meaning of pupil participation and, indeed, also to provide a challenge to how economic policies construct childhood (Dahlberg *et al.*, 1999). Nevertheless, this book also suggests that research in England into participation in the early years has a habit of missing out the reception class stage which, peculiar to this country, introduces children to the idea of a formal education system. These children often attend whole school assemblies and are primed for a sense of belonging to the school community and all it entails, such as the wearing of uniform and attendance throughout the day including lunchtime. This means that, despite the introduction of the foundation stage curriculum (DfEE, 2000) and the subsequent *Statutory Framework for the Early Years Foundation Stage* (DCSF, 2007), sometimes reception class children learn in a different context to nursery children. Guidance for participation and citizenship is often aimed either at the younger children in the nursery, in terms of informal strategies for involvement, or, alternatively, at the older, more articulate children who can engage through debate in school councils.

It is, thus, that a focus on the transitional period into statutory schooling is the theme for this book which explores the process of group identity building among the children in three reception or 'foundation 2'classes. To prepare for this, the next chapter examines why participation challenges perceptions of the education and care of children starting school. Then it looks at the role of researcher, teacher and child in realising participatory work.

Chapter 4

Participatory work at the start of school

Studying young children

As stated in the introduction to the book, the emerging paradigm for the sociology of childhood suggests that children should be studied as 'beings', rather than as 'becomings'. This is more challenging than it first sounds, in that child development, as viewed within the discipline of psychology, still dominates the construction of childhood that informs early childhood policy and curricula. This approach is based on a scientific 'othering' of children which upholds ideas of rationality, naturalness and universality. However, the emerging paradigm of study which encompasses children's own perspectives reflects postmodern ideas and opens the way for diversity in accounts of childhood which unsettles ideas of adult control and discipline. The new paradigm, therefore, is crucial to and dependent on an understanding of children's participation which presupposes that children already have a social self. This is in place of the previous models of childhood which regarded growing up and the move to adulthood as the process of socialisation.

The reception class setting, as signalled, is ground which seeks conceptual and practical clarity and is fertile for the study of competing discourses and wildly varying views of what young children are capable of. To study participation on this ground is to doubly challenge the approach of child development which would suggest that children at this point of transition are not yet competent to co-operate in the collective decision-making that participation encompasses. Thus, the study of participation in the reception class is better understood through application of the new paradigm of the sociology of childhood, that of 'being' which James and Prout (1997) outline. However, in order to provide a vocabulary to describe the beliefs which inform the child as 'being', it is useful to draw on James *et al.* (1998). This text provides a vocabulary and also possible routes for combining new and differing discourses. In this way, we can begin to make theoretical links between the real and also the conceptualised 'child', a potential contradiction which can pose difficulty for empirical research.

James *et al.* (1998, p.206) contend that the four categories for theorising childhood are that of the 'social structural', the 'minority group', the 'socially constructed' and the 'tribal' child. These categories also suggest collusions of meaning between them. For instance, whereas the social structural and minority group child both share a sense of continuity and universalism in terms of being fixed categories, the socially constructed and the tribal child are categories subject to greater interpretation and change. However, the tribal and minority group child share a sense of agency, whereas the socially constructed and social structural child share a determined sense of identity. The challenge of empirical study seems, therefore, to find ways in which these competing discourses can creatively combine and offer new explanations and solutions to the problems which are highlighted by research.

In the project described in this book, the attempt to move away from discourses of child development suggests a socially constructed perspective which views childhood as a provisional concept. Importantly, however, the boundaries of the project also allow access to the contrasting social structural viewpoint which does not problematise the notion of childhood. Additionally, since the task of developing children's agency and identity within a participation project can be seen as integral to each of James *et al.*'s (1998) four categories, so the prospect of the project moving between all four new discourses is made possible. At any rate, the theoretical interplay provides an opportunity for new insights into what it means to be a child, as opposed to becoming an adult.

In summary, therefore, new approaches in the study of childhood have questioned the universalising discourses, primarily psychological, which have been dominant in this area of research. The participation of children themselves in research has brought subjectivity to the notion of childhood which was previously lacking in the scientific discourses of child development. The challenge of this project was to make possible participation, within the new paradigm and from a postmodern perspective. To this end, the concept of the 'social child' (Woodhead, 1999, p.19) is useful, in that instead of emphasising *how* children become competent to participate it concentrates on '*the way* [my italics] children can be enabled to grow in competence through participation' (p.19). The key seems to be that the recognition of childhood as socially constructed opens the way for its reconstruction within a simultaneously postmodern and sociological paradigm. The story of this reconstruction is embodied by the story of doing empirical research with children.

The role of the researcher

As indicated previously, at the outset of this research project my role as researcher was conducted within employment as an early years support teacher working in the field of early years, disability and inclusion education for a local authority in the north of England. Because the project coincided with this teaching role, albeit with some distance from class teaching, the project adopted the action research methodology which was discussed in chapter one. Since supporting practitioner reflection and interpretation was also part of the support teachers' role to advocate participation in schools, it justified an action research project including the teachers as well as the children. In this way, the project aimed to clarify the support teacher's role as a properly inclusive one, supporting general teaching practice rather than supplying specific strategies for individual children.

Furthermore, in line with its theme, it was important that the research was conducted in a participatory way that involved the teachers and children in shaping its aims and course. Ely (1991, p.229) points out that, 'in Freire's (1970) terms, it is the social responsibility of qualitative researchers to avoid seeing and treating participants as passive objects and instead to work with them so that they become increasingly knowledgeable, active, responsible, and, therefore, increasingly liberated'. This was particularly important in an action research project which formed part of a work situation that would continue after the research finished. It meant that the aims of the research were potentially compatible with the stated aims of professional development which, for the support teacher, included providing an increasing amount of in-service training for practitioners and, for the class teacher, included teaching children with an ever increasing variation of abilities and backgrounds.

Thus, participation was built into the design of this project through the provision of joint meetings once a term with the class teachers. This allowed for planning and reviewing collaboratively away from the pressures of the classroom and a time to reflect together on the collected data. The design also involved the teachers in a project which suited their own class planning in the third term (described in the final chapter). This followed on from the activities which were planned and carried out primarily by the researcher. Thus the timetable for the research was as below.

Shulman's (2002) work separates the process of reflection into the content and form of pedagogical knowledge and identifies that knowledge of *what* to teach is different from knowledge of *how* to teach. This is useful for an understanding of how reflecting on participation in teaching practices focuses

Table 4.1 Research timetable

Visit	Term one	Term two	Term three
1	How children choose and share: watching	Making class decisions by voting	Children's reflections on photos
2	Children's concepts of fairness: listening	'Who Chooses' activity	*Playing Together* story
3	'Co-operative Faces' game	Children's reflections on 'Who Chooses'	Teacher projects and support
4	Co-operative games and voting pilot	Children taking photos	Teacher projects and support

reflection on teaching strategy generally, which may in turn result in greater innovation in the classroom. It was important for the project teachers themselves to understand and articulate the impact of their reflections and it was anticipated that the group meetings away from the classroom would facilitate this process. This also aimed to help with a sense of teacher agency and centrality in the research.

The role of the teacher

The teachers who took part in the project were central to its success. They opted into the project on the basis of their interest in developing participation in their classrooms and they agreed to the research and the researcher influencing the direction that this development took. From my perspective making initial observations, each teacher's 'regime' quickly began to take on a different character. Although all three teachers were clearly committed to exploring the children's views in their class, the way that they were approaching this varied greatly, according to their own strengths and abilities. For instance, in Allen Road reception class, the teacher, who was very experienced as a reception class teacher, was able to develop the children's emotional awareness and ability to understand friendship through the daily candlelit circle time which was held at the beginning of every day. The intimacy of this small class of 20 children gradually evolved to achieve a strong climate of trust, both in the teacher and each other. It was often during this session, with the guidance of the teacher, that children found the opportunity and ability to express their feelings about life.

In St Bede's reception class, the teacher was not experienced with the age group, having only taught in reception class for one year previously. However, this teacher was exceptionally creative in her teaching methods, using stories to develop the children's language and cognitive ability. This teacher took on an enabling role with the children, rarely directing them but instead posing questions for the children to reflect upon and discuss in an effort to help children arrive on their own at suitable decisions. She also explored emotion with them by attaching emotions such as 'happy' and 'sad' to events in the classroom, again with the aim of prompting the children to reflect on and articulate their own social behaviour.

In Cooper Road reception class, the teacher was also relatively new to teaching the reception class age group. However she was especially keen to develop the area of outdoor play for the children. They were involved each day in setting up and clearing away equipment which encouraged co-operative play and physical skills development. Added to this, they visited the local park each week. This teacher's style of teaching was that of a tutor, in that the children were given responsibility to help in the classroom but within a structure that made clear that the authority and leadership was primarily in the hands of the adult.

Table 4.2 Participatory practices

Teacher	Teaching strength	Teacher's role	Children's role
Allen Road	Confidence	Guide	Member
St Bedes	Communication	Enabler	Co-constructor
Cooper Street	Co-operation	Tutor	Helper

As the project progressed, in discussion with the teachers, I began to categorise their interests as representative of differing aspects of emerging features important for the development of children's participation. In other words, these teachers, all committed to the idea of children's participation, had particular and equally valid strengths and practices to offer to the project. These were each delivered through a particular style of leadership which in turn constructed the children in each classroom in different roles. This conceptualisation is represented by Table 4.2 above.

This framework will be referred to in the subsequent sections as an explanatory tool to discuss the ways in which children perceived their own identities within the classrooms. It should be noted that in practice the teaching strengths depicted above naturally overlap and reinforce each other. Therefore the assigning of a teaching strength to each teacher should only be seen as an analytical tool and relative starting point in the practice of all three strengths, both in the course of the project as well as in the course of their teaching careers. However, whilst the labelling of the teachers' strengths is in some ways reliant on the research theme, the categorisation of roles can clearly be evidenced from the research findings which are detailed in later chapters in relation to the themes which emerged from the children's comments and own observations.

The role of the child

Within the new paradigm for the study of childhood, as advocated by James and Prout (1997), the child must be viewed as the subject rather than the object of any research about her or him. Nevertheless, the difficulty which follows a paradigm shift is that of acknowledging and contextualising past beliefs and knowledge. For instance, despite promoting the concept of the 'social' child over 'developmentalism', Woodhead (1999) refers favourably to the well-known child development psychologist Jean Piaget. He acknowledges that one of Piaget's goals was to 'encourage greater respect for young children's ways of thinking and behaving' (p.19). Woodhead's tribute demonstrates that, whilst promoting new paradigms, it is possible to take account of what has gone before. Psychological approaches to children's development have also been enriched by combining the disciplines of psychology and cultural studies. Rogoff (2003) suggests that humans develop 'through their changing participation in the socio-cultural activities of their communities' (p.168). Importantly, she recognises that these communities also change and thus development cannot proceed in fixed ways. Furthermore, schools which are run by the dominant group in a society often provide activities for children that are decontextualised from their communities' endeavours.

Gilligan and Wiggins (1988) also employ perspectives which challenge psychological debates by presenting a feminist perspective on Piaget's notion of egocentric detachment, which simultaneously builds on yet reverses his thesis. Gilligan and Wiggins are concerned with identifying the origins of morality in early childhood and provide a critique on Piaget's idea that the individual is primarily egocentric. They assert (1988, p.135) that egocentric detachment is 'an avoidable result of a certain kind of morally alienating experience' rather than 'a paradigm case of development'. This important critique assumes that the child is primarily a social being who only loses the potential of this social understanding if isolated.

Gilligan (1988) also notes that this harmonises with Bowlby's (1969, 1973, 1980) theories of attachment. By observing children's response to separation from their mother, Bowlby came to see 'a capacity for love that was previously unimagined' (Gilligan, 1988, p.10). This was in direct contrast to the work of Freud (1914) and suggests that the danger of separation is the suppression and loss of this love rather than the memory and continuation of it into the present. This assumes, therefore, that children from an early age are capable of interacting with the people around them; of moving others and being moved by them. In addition to this, attachment relationships, which young children are already part of, have moral implications. Thus, instead of self-awareness as tied to detachment and independence from parents, it can be linked to 'a perspective on relationships that underlies the conception of morality as love' (Gilligan and Wiggins, 1988, p.115). This suggests that even the youngest children in school are capable of empathy and understanding another viewpoint, despite Piagetian ideas about their intrinsic egocentricity. It also explains the dual hazards of oppression and abandonment which children face by virtue of being born into a situation of inequality and adult connection (Gilligan and Wiggins, 1988, p.115). This new understanding of children's part in their own moral development can then inform the expectations, interpretations and adult guidance of young children's behaviour which make participation possible.

Gilligan's (1988) and Gilligan and Wiggins' (1988) writings centre on the view that the individualising of young children in the developmental paradigm denies them access to the communities of which they are an integral part. Schools aiming to exist alongside, and even represent, those communities must then consider how to combine a sense of development and belonging at one and the same time. Griffiths (1995), in outlining how feminisms affect 'the web of identity' (title page), believes that school policy can help children 'to understand the power of collectivity in the creation of their own identities' (p.122). Her view is that individual identity is only possible through membership of a community which in turn is continually reconstructing that identity (p.93). This mutual and interdependent process of change is not as benign as it sounds, in that the individual is not always aware of the social groups which create self-identity (p.120) and so control over its formation is necessarily limited.

This argument enhances the desirability for children to sense at least some degree of control within the immediacy of their classroom setting. This can then help to balance cultural with organisational issues, protect self-esteem and recognise the child's competence in the moral domain, as outlined previously by Gilligan and Wiggins (1988). Furthermore, the exercise of children's agency can be seen as intrinsic to, rather than separate from, mental development itself so that, rather than developmental concerns prescribing the level of children's competence to participate in the classroom, it may be the reverse.

Russell (1996, p.280), also exploring child psychology, defines agency as 'the ability to alter perceptual inputs at will'. In other words, the subject can distinguish between experiences that are caused by the world and the self and thereby begin to control the order in which one has those experiences. Russell (1996) also supports the notion that if children experience agency, there is no barrier to their perception of agency in other people. In other words, the idea that children can only acquire the ability to understand other people's point of view at a specific developmental stage is no longer valid. Instead, experience of agency *informs* that development, not the other way round.

However, Russell does not evade the observation that children do appear to pass through different stages in their ability to demonstrate empathetic understanding of others. But it is exactly that: the ability to *demonstrate* that is at issue; 'the control over the process of framing judgements' when asked to that the child has to refine. This is essentially a language task. In this way, Russell (1996) characterises the acquisition of theory of mind as 'a gradual, holistic dawning' rather than a set of discontinuous developmental stages. This argument has major implications for how we view children's capability. Crucially, Russell is stating that 'adequate mental development depends on adequate early agency' (p.2) which provides a solid argument for educators to take young children's participation very seriously indeed. With this in mind, we move from the role of the child in participatory work to consider the role of children's perspectives in the project.

Children's perspectives

As suggested in chapter one, the idea that children have one unified perspective, which can be discerned by research, undermines their diversity as a group and also their individual membership of communities, other than that of the school. Nevertheless, for the purpose of clarifying and illuminating the ideas of participation in the project, I considered that it would be helpful to focus on a particular child in each classroom and allow their perspective to provide a lens through which other children's responses were viewed. Importantly, these children were each perceived by their teachers and parents to be struggling with the process of settling into school life in the context of the reception classroom.

The focus child in Allen Road reception class was a boy who will be called Tom. He had also been referred to the service I worked for because of concerns about his behaviour and I was the support teacher responsible for monitoring and advising on his progress. Therefore he was at a stage 3 level of concern according to the *Code of Practice* (DfEE, 1994). Because of additional concerns about his care, social services were involved with his family. As a result of doubts about his mother's ability to care for him and his younger brother, he had recently started to live with his grandmother. Because of this he had also moved schools and therefore had attended a different nursery. There were varying reports about Tom's ability, since care issues had dominated his performance in nursery in terms of emotional behaviour.

The focus child in St Bede's reception class was a girl who will be called Abi. On entry to school she was reported by her mother to have developmental delay linked to extreme prematurity and a history of respiratory difficulties. She was reluctant to speak and found it difficult to conform to class routines and expectations of behaviour. She appeared socially isolated, though not necessarily unhappy in the classroom. Abi was an only child.

Finally, the focus child in Cooper Street reception class was a boy who will be called David. He was reported to have difficulty with peer relationships, in terms of over-dominance and refusal to share. He was an only child whose mother shared the school's concerns and was keen for advice about how to manage his behaviour at home as well as school. He was an able child who had also attended the school's nursery.

It was, thus, possible to identify in the foundations of the project an early and appropriate movement towards ascertaining the meaning of participation from a young child's viewpoint. This is perhaps akin to adopting the 'tribal' view of the child which James *et al.* (1998) describe as 'the empirical and potentially politicized version of the "social structural" child' (p.214). This reinforces a point made earlier, that the project was able to move between different conceptions of childhood and benefit from diverse theoretical standpoints. Thus, whilst participation had been formulated, with recourse to theories of democracy, as incurring a profoundly social dimension, it was not enough simply to impose these meanings onto children. Since they were also in the process of constructing hypotheses and making meaning in their daily lives, this needed to be reflected the process of defining participation too.

Summary

In this chapter, the project is detailed further and its rationale explained. The researcher's and teachers' roles have been shown as complementary to each other in the implementation of the project as action research and children's perspectives, through the representation of focus children, have been signalled as crucial to eventual interpretations of participation. Most importantly, discussion of childhood itself is undertaken and key perspectives defined.

It is significant that justification for the primacy of children's moral role in their own development is taken from psychological as well as political and philosophical texts. Nevertheless, it is the new paradigm for the sociology of childhood (James *et al.*, 1997) which is shown to inform the overall approach of the project. Thus, it is argued that the perspectives taken on children and childhood move between all the four categories which James *et al.* (1997) identify.

When trying to understand what children are capable of in moral terms, the developmental paradigm, which is currently dominant in professional approaches to children, is portrayed at best as a constraint and at worst as oppressive. The assumption that children are born into and become part of a moral dimension necessitates that they are viewed as exercising agency with a growing refinement in line with the growth of experience of interaction (Gilligan and Wiggins, 1988). Russell (1996) also provides evidence that children's experience of agency informs development rather than vice versa, as is commonly supposed in a developmental approach to childhood.

We must remember, however, that Gilligan and Wiggins (1988) also outline children's experience of inequality as unavoidable. With this in mind, it is to the theme of children's perspectives of their struggle to exercise agency within the new social environment of the classroom that we look next.

Chapter 5

What am I good at?

Introduction

This and subsequent chapters focus on the themes that evolved from children's comments and behaviour in the classroom. This material was collected through observations of and activities with the children. It was filtered through the analysis of the adults involved but, nevertheless, it helped to form a coherent picture of the issues which children in a reception class confronted in order to feel secure about their place in that environment. Thus, these themes are categorised under the headings of questions that children might ask themselves as they settle into school. In these themes, there is a deliberate movement from individual and expressive to social and structural aspects of reception classroom life. This aims to mimic the task of the child starting school, having to forge a new identity in a new social environment.

From the children's perspective, starting school often involved the issues of inequality and distribution of resources which were signalled in the last chapter. This was also made apparent by conversations with them about playing, choosing and sharing. Since discussion about these concepts needed contextualising to make sense to the children, it was best to refer to recent classroom incidents. In all three classes, children said that they made choices largely on the basis of liking, both activities and other children. Occasionally, more assertive 'wants' were expressed. However, although their responses suggested encouraging levels of emerging self-confidence, the answers given also reflected an adult view of the classroom, in that strategies for solving conflicts of interest were individualised and revolved around adult intervention. Thus, while children appeared comfortable with choosing activities for themselves, they were less skilled at solving disputes. The interviews often revolved around adult exhortations about sharing, which on the face of it were poor strategies for dealing with the issue of fair distribution of classroom resources. The next step, therefore, had to be to gain further insight of the reality, rather than the rhetoric of sharing in the classroom.

In order to signal this sense of reality, the next three chapters aim to show that inequality and redistribution, or sharing in children's eyes, are not just issues linked to knowing the rules, especially given the evident deficits in the way rules are disseminated to children. Instead, I suggest that, in children's eyes, the appropriation of resources is intrinsically linked to the senses of competence, loyalty and power which are discussed here and in the next two chapters. In this way, I contend that rules which govern issues of the sharing of resources in the reception class, and which are discussed in the subsequent chapter, rely primarily on issues to do with the confidence of individuals to relate to others. This is based on evidence that children's choices reflect issues of identity and belonging which form the core of the recognition theory of democracy as an ethic of social justice (Fraser, 1995).

Thus, the following chapters aim to provide an insight into how the two competing discourses of democracy discussed earlier, redistribution and recognition, interlink and build on each other in the reception class context. This will echo Honneth's (2002) view, also discussed earlier, that struggles over redistribution contain struggles for recognition precisely because they are symbolic of the socio-cultural ordering of the value of different activities. This, then, suggests that principles of recognition are important in the class-room, in terms of children's sense of self-worth, as a means of making sure that the sharing of resources is equitable.

Competence

Competence is a key term in debates related to children's participation. Questions of competence also form the hidden agenda behind the reluctance to discuss participation in relation to young children, for whilst a develop-mental view of childhood persists, the question of whether children of four and five years old have the ability to make valid and reasonable decisions must be questioned.

In terms of the perspectives on children's rights enshrined in the UNCRC cited in chapter three, a protectionist view encompasses the idea that rights can be upheld by adults on children's behalf until they are deemed competent enough to make decisions themselves, for instance on matters to do with their own health. Generally, this concept of competence is related, in legal terms, to age. In other words, the older a child, the less problematic becomes the notion of the responsibility of decision-making, as a rational activity. At the opposite end of the debate on children's rights, a liberationist perspective privileges children's competence to make decisions, suggesting that the absence of decision-making by children relates to a misplaced conception of childhood which has been appropriated by adults for sentimental reasons. This perspective regards childhood as 'a prison' which keeps children in an adult conception of the state of childhood (Holt, 1975).

Both of these polarised views contain important approaches for work with young children. Worldwide, children as a group do not have the power to exert rights of citizenship and, therefore, they are reliant on adults in many ways.

However, there are also numerous examples of situations where even young children take equal, if not more responsibility than adults in both macro- and micro-economic contexts and could be regarded as competent members of society. Nevertheless, to 'throw out the baby with the developmental bathwater' (Woodhead, 2000, p.124) could be to place inappropriate burdens of responsibilities on the heads of young children and it is important not to ignore the benefits of accommodating young children's desire for time and recreational space in which to grow and learn from the world. The dilemma is how to acknowledge this without denying that young children can be competent in ways that adults need to understand better than they do at present.

A solution to this dilemma, Kjorholt *et al.* (2005, p.178) argue, is that young children's competence is 'seen as dynamic and relational'. This means that competence, though viewed as constituted by the social space and practices of which they are a part, is nevertheless also seen as 'a dynamic concept referring to specific and differentiated forms of practices and skills' (p.178). Thus, to trace the children's own view of competence is perhaps a way to harness its transformative and dynamic possibility. It is also possible that, whereas Kjorholt *et al.* (2005, p.181) view competence 'not as a finished state related to independence but as an ability to relate', children in a reception class might suggest other contingencies from their perspective on this theme.

To explore this further, I suggest that we look at competence from Tom's viewpoint in Allen Road reception class. For Tom, it was possible to see that failure was a frightening prospect which made it safer to walk away from tasks which involved too many unreliable factors. However, it was also possible to see that his fear resided not just in perceptions of his own ability but also in the responses of others.

The activity which I want to describe at this point, in relation to Tom, is called 'Co-operative Faces' (see p.91). This game was designed to encourage co-operation between groups of four children in order to each complete a picture of a face. This meant that the children needed to work together to swap the pieces, so that each ended up with the pieces they needed for their own picture. This proved too difficult for Tom, who not only abandoned the task fairly quickly, but also openly rejected advances of friendship made by members of the group at circle time by saying that he didn't want to be anyone's friend. However, Tom had experiences which were different to many children in the class. Information about his home experiences bore out a disrupted picture of a child who had been moved to live with a grandparent because of maternal incompetence and neglect. On another occasion, taking on an adult perspective and turn of phrase, he was heard to comment: 'I cook me dinner on my own – I used to do it when I were your age.'

Tom was in possession of competencies which seemed unusual in the context of his peer group. He was unusually deft with language and nuances of expression. He made confessions which were poetic and demonstrated a reflective self-awareness. When discussing choices with him, this interaction occurred:

> T: And I hit my brother—
> C: **Did you? Oh right.**
> T: And I hit him in my bedroom—
> C: **Did you?**
> T: He's only a baby though, he's only a baby.
> C: **Really? Oh I see.**

Again Tom seemed burdened by an adult type of responsibility. However, importantly, he was using the opportunity to unburden himself in a medium he was competent with, that is, language.

The interesting thing is that, whilst Tom was able to express himself effectively, as was also evident in the other activities which are described in subsequent chapters, yet he seemed unable to recognise and take pride in this competence. He also found it hard to demonstrate self-confidence, despite his ability to look after himself by cooking. This seems to lend weight to Kjorholt *et al.*'s (2005) argument that competence is about the ability to relate to others. Tom was disadvantaged in the class because his experiences were not common to the other children, although they were recognised to some degree by the adults. It was because of this recognition that he felt able to express himself so competently, although unfortunately he seemed unable to recognise his own competence as yet. Instead, he felt relatively unsafe with the other children and struggled with a sense of social isolation, which put his own abilities at risk.

Interestingly, Kjorholt *et al.*'s (2005) social meaning of competence also seems to be foregrounded from the perspective of Abi in St Bede's reception class. Abi had been initially identified as having difficulties relating to developmental delay as a result of a premature birth and early respiratory problems. Nevertheless, this 'delay' in development initially manifested itself as an unwillingness to conform to social expectations within the class. Although it proved to be the social dimension of peer group which she particularly struggled with, unlike Tom, she couldn't express this eloquently. She was frequently and overtly shunned by other children and described to me as lacking in friends. Nevertheless, on one occasion when she was criticised by a female peer for interfering with the tidying up, she responded by saying that she wouldn't invite the group of girls involved to her party. In this way, she learnt very quickly how to defend herself in the effective coinage of the classroom, since this class traded in invitations and stories of ballet lessons after school.

However, like Tom, when it came to group activity, Abi often declined to join in despite the beginnings of friendship with another child in the classroom. On one occasion she refused to participate in acting out a story she had helped to dictate and it seemed as if this level of performance was, for her, a step too far. Thus, on this occasion, it may have been that Abi's reluctance to 'act out' was not just a social phenomenon but also about her reliance on one particular medium of storytelling which she didn't yet feel ready to change. This is a different stance to saying that she could not do it or was not capable of doing it and suggests that we need to constantly question the motivation for children to demonstrate ability.

Dyer (2002, p.74), writing about emotional intelligence, says that children need to feel good about themselves, not only in the sense of knowing that they are capable of great bravery and taking care of another child, but also 'in the sense of being found lovable, no matter what'. She goes on to say that this is something the children sometimes seem to have little control over. In this light it is hardly surprising that Tom and Abi, with their different disadvantages, nevertheless both viewed their peer group with reserve. Competence for them was defined by others.

Mastery

Kjorholt *et al.*'s (2005) social view of competence, which has been well illustrated by Tom and Abi, can be further embellished by a perspective from Cooper Street which demonstrates how children negotiate the mastery of formal skills. The word 'mastery' is used here deliberately to differentiate between the relational view of competence described earlier and the more typically (and intrinsically gendered) view of school achievement as the ability to learn and apply abstract skills and knowledge.

The majority of children in Cooper Street reception class had been together in the school nursery and seemed to be comfortable within the group. This may have contributed to the noticeable frequency of peer consultation about formal literacy and numeracy skills. Shared conversations about the ability to form letters and numbers were frequently overheard and helpful tips were passed on. For example: 'I can do a nine' was responded to by another child with: 'It's like a six upside down'. In this way the competence to perform tasks set by the teacher was nurtured co-operatively amongst groups of children, though there also remained a high degree of reliance on teacher authority to sort out disputes. Thus, this class provided an interesting mixture of peer group ease combined with views of the teacher as a tutor figure (see p.43) and school knowledge as distinctive currency of the classroom.

In all the classes, it was often number play which provided the most prevalent demonstration of children testing their sense of competence in relation to a school environment. The 'Who Chooses' activity (see p.91) provided children with an unexpected opportunity (on my part) to discuss numerical significance. This activity, which is described in more detail in the next chapter, incurred the children each being given six stickers and asked questions about decisions in their daily lives. The 'six-ness' of the stickers was commented on at Allen Road by comments such as: 'I've got one, two, three, four, five, six' and as each sticker was used the stickers left were counted up. This interest in number was also echoed in conversations prompted by the activity which stimulated both the children's playfulness as well as their knowledge of greater numbers. For instance, in this example of a conversation between three children:

'I got five sisters and I got two brothers.'
'I got six sisters and six brothers.'
'I got forty one.'

Certain children at Allen Road also showed concern with the accurateness of spelling, as well as that of number, through the 'Who Chooses' activity. For instance, Iona took on an instructional role in the activity by making sure that I had spelt the children's names correctly.

However, despite these examples of children playing with and controlling the knowledge associated with school learning, the children at Allen Road repeatedly showed that verbal communication created barriers for them when dealing with adults in school. Although Tom wanted to have his voice heard by ensuring that the tape recorder was switched on when he started to speak, other children often resorted to sign language to get their meaning across. When I asked Tamsin if she was going to give Laura a turn on her bike, she replied with: 'That many times' showing me four fingers. I questioned her meaning: 'That many times? What? Round the playground?' This was answered haltingly with: 'We going to ... gi' it t' Laura when we finished.' It seemed that the interface of adult question and child response was often disjointed and revealed fault lines and fragmentation, especially when children were exercising a high level of agency and competence in their play activities.

However, it was not just the children at Allen Road who found adult language and questioning irrelevant to the immediacy of their activities. It was an exception that children's responses showed interest in themselves as learners, as in the example of Janey at St Bede's, questioned about her choice to do a painting: 'I thought I was making a picture, then I put colours on it.' Janey knew she was thinking; knew what thought was and how actions can change intentions. However, this type of competence was mainly difficult to capture and the use of language as a mode of thinking remained a barrier between adult and child, suggesting that language is not an ideal medium for adults and children to communicate with each other, particularly when it demands an answer to a question.

Because of this barrier, visual methods of communication with children take on additional significance in research with children. In their work on the mosaic approach, cited in chapter three, Clark and Moss (2001) suggest that children's photographs can provide a focus for expression and communication with adults. Children's competence with regard to the visual image is important here and Ennison and Smith's view (2000) consolidates the idea that the images children produce put them in charge of the concepts behind them. This then incurs reinforcement of their ability, not only to produce the image but also to own its meaning.

These assertions of children's competence with visual media were well supported by the use of photographs in the project (see p.54–58). A significant majority of children were able to remember their own image several weeks after the photos were taken and, furthermore, they could make a good guess at which photos belonged to whom, showing a high level of knowledge of each other. This surprised me, as the photos were often taken at busy times and did not seem to incur much forethought. The question the children were asked before they took a photo was: 'What do you like at school?' The responses could be categorised into those who chose friends, individual and groups, and those who chose activities, in and out of the classroom. The photos themselves showed the child's perspective forcefully in terms of relative size; for instance, at St Bede's, the 'Iron Man' model seems enormous and the close-up of the trucks highly engaging (see Figures 5.1 and 5.2).

In this way a photo can communicate the child's perspective to the adult even prior to further joint reflection on the images. However, it was at the point of the reflective activity that the competence of the children to interpret and code their images became most prominent.

When Colleen at Cooper Street was asked to choose which one of the two photographs she'd taken (Figures 5.3 and 5.4) she liked best, she immediately chose Figure 5.4 because she liked the detail of her friend's belt in the picture. As an adult, I'd assumed that she would choose the photo which seemed to me to be the better composition, in terms of clearly portraying her friends' faces. Arguably, however, the opportunity to review her images enabled her to recollect, refine and express her 'true' interest. It was also a specific detail

Figure 5.1 Iron Man

Figure 5.2 Trucks

Figure 5.3 Colleen 1

Figure 5.4 Colleen 2

in a photograph (Figure 5.5) which was commented on by Ahmber at Cooper Street.

Rather than the water tray, which I had assumed to be the subject of the photo, it was the milk carton in the far top right-hand corner of the photo which excited Ahmber's attention. The carton appeared to represent for him one of the freedoms of this classroom: that you were allowed to collect your milk and carry it around with you to your chosen activity.

In this way, the photos provided children with the opportunity to initiate and determine conversation. The images were less complicated than verbal language at the same time as supporting it. This allowed almost all of the children a sense of competence which was not reliant on adult-determined mastery. Nevertheless, it is difficult to deny the importance to children of mastery of the knowledge and skills learnt at school. They know when they enter the school environment that certain knowledge and skill belongs there and, alongside evidence of the desire to establish themselves as social beings, there is also evidence of their desire to acquire this currency. For some children this acquisition seems easier than for others and I suggest that an understanding of adults, rather than other children, may be a key to this. To illustrate this point we must meet David, the focus child at Cooper Street.

Figure 5.5 Ahmber

You mean working as a team?

In Cooper Street reception class, the focus child, David, had been identified as finding peer group social relationships difficult but, in contrast to Tom and Abi, he demonstrated self-assurance in his understanding of situations in the classroom and seemed confident to deal with them, even when this made him unpopular. My assessment was that David knew how to deal with these situations because he understood the answers adults like to hear. For instance, he told his teacher that he had played 'nicely' at playtime and he explained to me that he would give a train to another child who wanted to play with him. However, when I asked him if that was hard (meaning emotionally hard), he assumed that I thought that separating the trains was a technically hard (as in difficult) operation. He demonstrated how the trains came apart quite easily and said, 'No, you just take them off like that'.

It was interesting that David and I misunderstood each other in this particular context because his level of competence in the classroom, in terms of self-confidence, seemed to emanate primarily from his ability to act as a translator of adult meanings. This he often did for the other children, so that while he tended to control peer group play he was able to mediate when the teacher struggled to get meanings across to the class. He advised his peers about the teacher's strategy, saying: 'Whoever says "me" they don't get it' and he filled in gaps in instructions during a PE lesson when the teacher struggled to explain sufficiently. Though David controlled these situations, my impression was that he did so because he was familiar with adult communication. Indeed, his mother reported that she thought his status as an only child in the family was contributing to his occasional intolerance of and dominance amongst his peer group.

In fact, despite his dominance, David was a very useful member of the class, as his ability to gather meanings from adults and convey this to his peers was often helpful. When I attempted to explain the concept behind the 'Co-operative Faces' game to a group of children, David helpfully suggested that working together was 'like working as a team', a reference which the others understood well in the context of a recent class discussion about a much publicised England rugby team victory. This ability to communicate was a competence which David knew he possessed and which gave him his confidence despite what adults perceived as warranted unpopularity with his peers. Unlike Tom, he was secure in this sense of competence and didn't need to have as much invested in peer group relationships.

In each of the three classes it was possible to identify a child who, similar to David, took on the role of translator of adult language and communication. This highlights the work of Donaldson (1978) and Russell (1996), who have both identified the crucial role of language in the emergence of children's ability to demonstrate theory of mind and thus understand that others think. As discussed in chapter four, Russell points out that it is important to distinguish *demonstration* of theory of mind, which is reliant on children's language skill, from *understanding* of theory of mind which is reliant on agency, not language. Nevertheless, when a child can translate 'adult-speak' into something understandable for his or her peers, it suggests that he or she is 'aware of language as a distinct system' (Donaldson, 1978, p.93) and is therefore able to separate 'what is said from what is done' (p.93). Donaldson goes on to suggest that this development of consciousness is closely linked to the growth of the intellect, the higher intellectual powers being dependent on the child's control over his or her thinking. This can only happen as the child becomes aware of thinking and at the base of this awareness lies the sense of agency which Russell (1996) refers to. Thus, children, like David, who mediate between adults and peers in the classroom are those who have the strongest sense of their own ability and this sense of agency, expressed as competence, enables them to appreciate the agency of others and therefore the misunderstandings which they are able to rectify. This strong sense of agency, underpinned by emotional security, is crucial to the usefulness of language, which may suggest why Tom couldn't use his language skill to the same effect as David in the classroom.

Another example of this ability to translate adult-speak occurred at Allen Road when I asked a group: 'Who chooses what you do at school?' One of the children said in reply: 'My mum takes me to school' which prompted Jenny to clarify my question, saying to her peer: 'That's in the morning when we come to school, but we're thinking about what we choose, aren't we?' Thus Jenny took on a role which I was reluctant to assume in the 'research situation', that is the role of tutor. She had mastered not only the truer intention of my question but also the strategy behind the activity which enabled her to interact and help another. Emma at St Bede's also showed her understanding that adult help is not always possible or desirable, by indicating to the other children around the craft table that she could help them with the tape they were struggling with. Thus she took on a role, not so much of a translator of adult language, but more fundamentally as a translator of an adult's underlying meaning, in that she recognised and conveyed to her peers that the adult in this context wanted children to develop independence and self-help skills. Thus it was key children in each class who were able to demonstrate not only school knowledge but also a sense of competence which encompassed knowledge of adult intent in an adult-controlled world. In one example, Andrew at St Bede's was heard to say: 'Why can't there be 201 tables and 201 chairs?' and later: 'When I grow up I think I'll buy this school.'

However, although the activity 'Co-operative Faces' aimed to develop children's ability, as David suggested, to work as a team, in all classes, it was adult control of the game which ironically engendered better levels of co-operation. Thus, when the children were told that the completion of the activity would be timed, they became more efficient at co-operating with each other. This suggested that the competence to co-operate in this activity, devised by an adult, was in fact closer to the school-determined competence observed when children shared their knowledge of letters and numbers than to the children's own attempts to socialise and make friends.

Furthermore, the greater the task element of the exercise was explained, the more efficient the co-operation became, guiding the children's behaviour, giving them a sense of common ground and leaving less to them to work out for themselves. This suggests that co-operation, like other competencies expected in the classroom environment, benefits from being addressed directly rather than left to chance. Echoing the gendered meaning of 'mastery' this seemed particularly true of working with boys in the classrooms who, like David, tackled co-operation as another aspect of the adult agenda to be understood and acted upon. When he clarified with me: 'You mean working as a team?' he was confident that, having identified what I meant, he would be able to accomplish this new demand.

Kjorholt et al.'s (2005, p.178) dynamic view of competence, which is dependent on 'the elaboration of particular practices in a specific context' and therefore constantly changing, does allow for relational skills to be acquired in this taught way to match the context within which they occur, a context which Gilligan and Wiggins (1988) suggest may also imply a gender difference in experiences of empathy and the way boys and girls develop relational skills. They cite Hoffman's (1977) research which suggests that, whilst both boys and girls are equally capable of identifying with and understanding the feelings of others, girls tend to 'experience [my italics] the other's feelings' (p.124). Regardless of the essentialist gender debate here, the pedagogical implications are that a didactic method of teaching social skills needed for co-operation may have added significance for children who don't easily experience empathy. Thus, an overtly didactic method of knowledge acquisition tends to conceive of competence as involving 'mastery' of skills, portraying ability and inferring that competence itself is individualised and innate. This matches the view of ability which was illustrated by the children's desire to demonstrate their knowledge of numbers and letters. However, the successful use of a more didactic approach in the 'Co-operative Faces' game suggests that 'mastery' can also be practised on relational skills and arguably play a part in education for co-operation as well as for competition. This means that boys like David, who like explanations, become more competent at relating to others in the recognition of common aims.

Summary

In this chapter, it has been suggested that children's sense of themselves as competent in the early days at school relies on their emotional and cognitive resources to relate to other children in the classroom. This definition of competence builds on the work of Kjorholt et al. (2005) and highlights the day-to-day difficulties faced by Tom and Abi. The most settled class of the three had been together in the school nursery and showed evidence of what I have called the 'mastery' of school knowledge more frequently than the other classes. In general, however, language used by adults to children has been identified as a barrier to learning which the use of photos helped to bridge, by giving children more control over the communication (literally) of their point of view.

David and the other children who acted as translators of adult meanings demonstrated a high degree of competence and confidence in the classroom which, it is suggested, demonstrates frequent exercise of agency in their lives. To a lesser extent, many of the children in the classes were engaged in building a sense of competence in this way and, bearing in mind that Russell (1996) suggests that agency allows the subject to control the order in which one has experiences, agency was visible both in conversational play with school-based knowledge as well as in the discussion of their photos. These examples all showed growing ability to deal with the new and external experience provided by entry to school.

Finally, however, it is suggested that some children, like David, benefited from being taught co-operation as a discrete, rather than an incidental, set of skills. This allowed them the same sense of 'mastery' gained from tackling school knowledge. Nevertheless, it is the relational competence, as evident in the formation of children's relationships, that has been argued as the strongest sign of the development of children's agency, so the next chapter examines in more depth how children approach the question 'Who's my friend?'

Chapter 6

Who's my friend?

Loyalty and love

It was discussed in chapter five that the ability to relate to each other was viewed by children as akin to a survival skill in the reception class environment. Even in the case of David, who was confident in his ability to relate to adults, his teacher suggested that the desire to play together with another child was stronger than the desire to compete. When competitiveness threatened to end his play, it was usually brought back on track by both the children involved. Paley (1999) suggests that the desire to make friends is so strong that it often dominates even the need to compete. Relating to examples of numerous experiences with young children, she says that 'the early instinct to help someone is powerful' (p.129). Penn (1998, p.6) also says that there was evidence in her research that children felt it was important to 'be part of a group and experience solidarity with other children'.

Nevertheless, the evidence of this project also suggests that children have a broad view of who their allies are in the classroom environment. The necessity to make friends with peers was accompanied by a demonstration of deep loyalty and love towards the significant people in their home life. These loyalties seemed to enter into school life more than was immediately apparent and provided a presence of emotional support to children as they embarked on the newer, less secure and more slippery liaisons in the classroom. This deep sense of loyalty demonstrated that, from the child's point of view, the reception classroom was indivisible from the rest of their life. It also reflected the 'epiphanies of the ordinary' which Bruner (1983, p.134) identified as children's everyday routines with parents which 'embed the child's communicative intentions in a cultural matrix'.

The 'Who Chooses' activity (see p.91) allowed children to express their loyalties and sense of belonging eloquently. This activity was used with groups of four children at a time. They were each given a sheet with three shapes symbolising different 'actors' in their lives and then asked a set of six questions about who makes the decisions about what happens to them in the course of their day. The children were then asked to respond to the questions by placing a sticker in a shape on their sheet. This allowed for the children to decide on the way to interpret the activity as well as to gain support and ideas from each other in the process.

As well as stimulating talk about number, as illustrated in chapter five, the 'Who Chooses' activity tended to make the stickers into powerful tokens of approval. Thus, the children participating became aware of key people whom they wanted to reward, including themselves, as they awarded the stickers in answer to each of the six questions about who made decisions in the course of their day. For instance, at Allen Road, Mary said: 'I need to get a sticker for [Teacher] – I want to – she says all the things what we can do.' At Cooper Street, Janey asserted: 'I like to choose my mum and dad.' In this way the children interpreted the activity as a demonstration of their approval of key people in their life. Similarly, at St Bede's, Amy awarded her stickers to her disabled brother saying: 'I want to put these both in here because I love my brother.'

Perhaps not surprisingly, Tom was especially sensitive to the effects of this activity as a means not only of showing his approval, but also of showing his need to be approved of by adults. Thus, he said about the choice of TV programmes in his home: 'I choose my nan-nan's... she picks her things and I watch them.' This corresponded to an assertion that he liked the teacher to tell him what to do. It also matched his change of mind in the 'Who Chooses' activity that, instead of his own choice, it was the teacher who told him what to do at school. When Danny, at Allen Road, nominated his dad as the person who made all the decisions about his day, saying that his dad told him 'to play with the animals', Tom similarly announced that his dad made decisions about his daily life. The striking point here was that neither Danny nor Tom were living with their fathers, so the promotion of their fathers to positions of such influence in their lives was regarded as an example of wishful thinking. Certainly, it further illustrated the power of this activity for children to express love, loyalty and empathy towards significant people in their lives.

The 'Who Chooses' activity also served as a vehicle for some children to express their own self-confidence. The issue of ownership of the stickers emerged as significant in all the classes with the comments: 'Can we take them home?', 'Are you allowed to take them?' and 'Whose are these?' Thus a natural elision was created between ownership of the resources and the agency exercised in making decisions. David was one of just two children in his class who thought that four out of the six decisions discussed were made by him. He was able to view events from an adult perspective and, unlike Tom, showed confidence in the approval of adults. During the activity he commented on the responses to the questions in his group. He pointed out that two children shared the same pattern of stickers. This appeared to be another demonstration of his desire to relate to adults in preference to peers, not just at home, but also in the classroom.

Like David, there were children in each class who said that they were the ones who made the significant decisions about what happened to them during the day. It was noticeable that the influence of these children often spread to the others in their group, so that the response 'I choose' became more frequently asserted by other children in the same group, as the activity progressed. This suggested that confidence, as well as conformity, might be catching when children engage in expressive activities. This builds a strong case for encouraging group work to include peers with varied levels of self-confidence. At St Bede's, many children declared themselves as choosers and Amy made further connections between decision-making and power, by saying: 'Mostly it's mums and dads who choose because they're bossy boots.'

The exception to the strong sense of individual agency in this class was Carrie, a triplet, who regularly said that she and her siblings took turns to choose what they had for breakfast and what they watched on television. Her sense of individual agency seemed therefore equally balanced with the needs of others at home. Whilst this finding appears to support findings of a study by Lewis *et al.* (1996, cited by Dunn and Brown, 2001, p.97) that the number of siblings positively correlates with the rate of success at mind-reading tests, it is important to consider that only child David also consistently demonstrated ability to 'mind-read' adult intentions and meanings. This would therefore refute the developmental thesis that 'only' children are disadvantaged in this way. Russell (1996) could be used to explain this discrepancy, with the suggestion that it is the experience of agency that is the most crucial aspect of the capacity to form relationships. Thus if children experience agency, there is no barrier to their perception of agency in other people. As Dunn and Brown (2001) suggest, questions which link culture, emotion and cognition are 'among the most difficult but central issues for developmental psychologists' (p.100).

The importance of care

The question in the 'Who Chooses' activity which presented the most puzzling expression of loyalty was: 'Who chooses what you do at school?' This was overwhelmingly answered with a sticker in the parents' shape. I had expected that most children would say that their teachers decided what they did at school but, in the event, this was the exception rather than the rule. In the light of this intimate connection of the classroom with children's home lives, I would argue that a strong consideration of the ethics of classroom practices becomes all the more apparent and that Sevenhuijsen's (1998) 'feminist ethics of care' is an appropriate ethical position for an early years setting to adopt. This position offers one explanation of the children's response to the question cited, as it infers that significant relationships are not just important, but also intrinsic to the individual. The children's response, therefore, could imply that the family relationships, which were brought to the foreground by the previous questions, do, in fact, remain the most significant connections for the child, even when they are separate from home and geographically stranded in the classroom.

Sevenhuijsen's concept of ethics is concerned more with 'responsibilities and relationships rather than rules and rights' (Dahlberg and Moss, 2005, p.74) and fits well with the project because it challenges the view of the individual as a distinct entity and instead conceives of her or him as involved in relationships which incur unexpected happenings and ambiguous outcomes. This ethical scheme assumes the idea of 'a self which is continually in the process of being formed' (Sevenhuijsen, 1998, p.56). Furthermore, this scheme challenges the pursuit of independence and autonomy, which is often prioritised by education, and replaces it with a feminist commitment to deal with differences within the self as well as within social groups. This is made possible because strangeness and knowability are conceived of as related to each other. Thus, Sevenhuijsen's (1998) view of self illuminates the findings in chapter five, which suggest that children view success in social relationships, both with adults and other children, as essential to their own success in the classroom environment.

Sevenhuijsen (1998) also suggests, as Young (2000) does, that aiming for compromise in decision-making may be more closely linked to social justice than aiming for Habermas's (1984, 1987) ideal of consensus. However, an ethics of care does not promote the idea of cultural relativism, but simply the idea that people should recognise their own cultural assumptions. Sevenhuijsen suggests that, in the end, moral knowledge will be limited by how much the moral critic can consider. Her 'ethics of care' also concurs with the position on participatory democracy put forward by Young (2000), in that recognition of difference provides the vital ingredient for communication based on a premise of equality. Young emphasises that styles of communication should not become barriers to listening to what people have to say. She suggests that rhetoric is the way that messages are constructed and conveyed in a manner which is 'appropriate to the particular context and audience to which we are speaking' (p.68). In other words, the medium is equal to the message and vice versa. This celebration of difference as a positive feature of participatory practice suggests that, despite any developmentally defined limitations of language ability, children already have a voice in their relationships with adults which should be taken seriously. Furthermore, they are active in forming those relationships both with adults and each other, a point reinforced in chapter four by discussion of the work of Gilligan and Wiggins (1988) who suggest that children create and sustain connections with others through the experience of attachment which then 'generates a perspective on relationships that underlies the conception of morality as love' (p.114).

Gilligan and Wiggins (1988) also state that 'strong feelings and clear principles are dependent on "authentic" relationships' (p.118). Alongside Bruner's 'epiphanies of the ordinary' (1983), this provides a further interpretation of the children's response by suggesting that not only feelings but also thoughts and values relate firmly to familiar adults. Thus from the child's perspective, the domain of the classroom may be no different from that of the home in its subjection to parental influence. It may be, then, that children acquire appreciation of the teacher's privileged position in school, in relation to that of their parents, at a much slower rate than we tend to assume.

Brooker (2002) further illuminates the theme that children utilise previous experience by explaining that, to make sense of school, children are carrying the beliefs and values of their parents at the same time as they are subject 'to the beliefs and expectations of their teachers' (p.154). In some cases this means that children are 'living in two worlds' rather than living a continuous experience between the two. Clearly this could then compromise their ability to translate one experience to the other. However, my own research suggests that the potential conflict of these two worlds might be mediated or alleviated by children's belief in their parents' influence on what they do in school. Clearly, this is an area for more research, but it would be interesting to see if there is a correlation between the children whom Brooker identified as 'living in two worlds' and children who recognised the power of the teacher in school rather than that of their parents.

The definition of familiar people by children in the 'Who Chooses' activity revealed that brothers, sisters and grandparents all played significant parts in their lives. They felt unconstrained by the format of the sheet which offered only themselves, parents and teachers as decision-makers and they felt able to offer other alternative decision-makers as they saw appropriate. Although the researcher was the questioner in this activity, the children seemed able not only to respond through the use of the stickers, but also to use the opportunity for expanding the narrative about their relationships with others. At Allen Road, Johnny said: 'I only play with boys. If all the girls were here, I'd play with myself.' He also explained that he chose TV programmes for his little brother. In this way the 'Who Chooses' activity became an expressive tool which provided a multi-faceted perspective on the process of children's relationship-building in, as well as out of, school.

Returning to Tom at Allen Road, we are reminded that not all children experience the security of love and care at home. As a result, Tom's experience of familial relationships betrayed one-sidedness. He frequently injected comments about dying and killing into discussions, expressing his anger in narrative form, such as in this example: 'Once there was a little rabbit and the girl killed him and then she said ***.' In another of his narratives, it was a 'baby' that suffered at the hands of those older and more powerful. Sadly, his behaviour seemed to indicate that awareness of the shortcomings of adult responsibility had become a burden which needed to be expressed negatively in his relationships in the classroom. For instance, he found it difficult to share a two-seater bike with another child and he told the other children at circle time that he didn't want to be friends with them. Nevertheless, he also tried to kiss Calum when playing outside and when Calum resisted said: 'Doesn't your mum kiss you?'

Tom's contradictory behaviour with regard to friendship with his peers needed careful handling by the teacher and she demonstrated understanding towards Tom by telling the other children that she was 'extra nice to people who are grumpy'. This helped to alleviate the bad feeling that Tom's defiantly anti-social 'I'm not going to be anyone's friend' provoked in the other children. Tentatively, the other children followed her guidance and Tom began to play with peers more successfully. At St Bede's, Abi, like Tom, initially sought isolation and suffered from peer group exclusion. Emma told me in a matter-of-fact way 'She's got no friends' and indeed Abi seemed to endorse this through her choice of play, rejecting social play in preference for the craft table. However, unlike Tom, Abi did not appear to carry a burden of responsibility for relationships; she merely engaged in them at a level she felt comfortable with. As the first term progressed she started to play outside with Elsa and by the third term she was better able to articulate her friendships.

Whereas Abi's progression towards friendship could be viewed as the effect of adapting, at her own pace, to peer pressure, her classmate Keir's response to the environment was more akin to that of Tom. Keir also needed to tell stories in which monsters and aliens dominated. This storytelling seemed to be a response to, and also prevented engagement with, the demands of others, especially adults. It seemed as if he was stuck in the identity of the 'naughty boy' talking about monsters and that this was more familiar territory than making friends. During the 'Who Chooses' activity, in which children reflected on who made decisions for them during a typical day, both Abi and Keir took the activity in unexpected directions; Keir put the stickers provided on his shirt, rather than the paper, a clear expression of non co-operation and Abi used the sticker as a symbol to represent the teacher visiting her house. When asked: 'Who chooses what you do at school?' she placed her sticker in her parents' shape on the sheet and explained, 'Mrs Baker came to my house'. This showed that the activity was able to be symbolic of a variety of different expressive statements.

Playing at playing together

There remains one key observation on the process of children building alliances, which was reinforced by the research methods used with them. This was most noticeable at Cooper Street, the class which appeared to comprise more settled peer relationships. Thus, on three occasions in this class, the name of another child was substituted for an activity. When, at circle time, the children were invited to state something they love (*doing* being implied), several children said 'I love [child's name]'. On another occasion, when I asked a child, 'What do you like playing with?' the answer was given as 'Ahmber'. Finally, when Toby was asked, 'Why did you choose the playdough?' he replied:

'Because Jake came and played with the playdough.' In these three examples we can see that *what* to play and *who* to play *with* had much the same meaning.

At St Bede's, the children in the earlier stages of friendship formation, as compared with those at Cooper Street, showed signs of deference to each other, as most children answered the question: 'Who chooses *what* you play?' with the name of a friend rather than suggesting that they might be the choosers themselves. Acquisition of a playmate in this case, as at Cooper Street, rated higher than a demonstration of independent agency. Arguably, at Allen Road, it was the role of the teacher as guide that lessened the currency of specific friendships, so that, even though Tom declared that he didn't want to be friends with anyone in the class, several children nevertheless put themselves forward to befriend him. In this way, at Allen Road, the acquisition of friends, though as important as in the other classes, was less individualised and feelings aired during circle time allowed for friendships to be controlled by the group as a whole, with the teacher as arbiter.

This tendency at Allen Road towards what we could call 'emotional literacy' was also apparent in a conversation a visiting colleague had with Annie. Annie invited my colleague to paint with her saying: 'We can do it together – this painting – both together.' When my colleague reinforced this suggestion by saying: 'I like doing this together', Annie saw this as an opportunity to talk about arguments between her separated parents. She concluded this conversation with:

> It'll be good now cos they're talking – talking to each other and not shouting. I hate it when they're shouting – that's not good friend's, is it; when you shout and you mean it?

This suggests that where the nature of friendship was a daily part of the teacher's concern, the classroom became a place where the children were able to analyse not only their own interactions, but also those of the people they were close to.

Hutter (1978, p.115), drawing on Aristotle's discussion of friendship, writes that all human associations are forms of friendship, 'even if only imperfectly'. This suggests that the process of forming allies is central to establishing one's place in a new social setting. Nixon (2004) also discusses Aristotle's *Nicomachean Ethics* and points to the distinctions of different kinds of friendship. Thus friendship may be provisional and strategic, as well as virtuous. The project suggests that children's actual alliances in the classroom are in early stages of formation and are based largely on pleasure and that the strongest alliances for the children in the study were with family members. These bonds were brought into the classroom with them in a tangible way and seemed to influence their subsequent relationships. They signified a demonstrable aspect of children's active ability to relate to other people.

Writing from a psychological perspective, Dunn and Brown (2001, p.99) echo Russell's (1996) assertions that children's social understanding can be noted through their role play and conversations before they can succeed in more scientific, formal assessments of theory of mind. This suggests that, even from a psychological perspective, children can demonstrate continuity in the development of their social understanding which is often overlooked. Thus they should be regarded as active partners in relationships with their peers as well as their parents, as Gilligan and Wiggins (1988) suggest. Nevertheless, it also seems important that children are given guidance, as well as opportunities, on how to make best use of their social understanding in a new setting. At Allen Road, with the example of Annie, we saw the benefits of this approach to children's learning; there was a daily circle time every morning during which children felt able to discuss matters arising from their home lives and thereby make sense of those connections in the classroom. This also seemed to help children like Tom who struggled to form the alliances in the classroom which might have helped to ease his sense of responsibility at home.

Despite the importance of parents as allies, familiar adults in the classroom did not seem to be perceived as allies in the same way. Teachers in particular were perceived more as leaders and rule-makers who could be called upon to sort out disputes. This was particularly so at St Bede's and Cooper Street, though the relationship of Allen Road's teacher with her class seemed more complex. This fits with the identified roles of these teachers as enabler, tutor and guide. Whilst teachers at Allen Road and St Bede's identified development of self-esteem and communication skills as important gains for the children in the project, the teacher at Cooper Street also highlighted that the project had given her 'an insight into what is happening in the classroom in how children relate to each other', as well as how her practice facilitated or hindered these relationships. This, she added, meant that the children would increase their independence from adults in the classroom.

Summary

This chapter suggests that, although peer relationships are in formation in the reception classroom, nevertheless, it is the family relationships which mostly lend emotional support to children whilst they are in school. This was demonstrated through responses to the 'Who Chooses' activity, in which children expressed loyalty and love towards a range of significant people in their lives, mostly outside the classroom. However, children who saw themselves as important decision-makers in their own lives were able to influence other children in their group to think in this way.

The importance in an early childhood institution of an 'ethics of care' (Sevenhuijsen, 1998) has therefore been asserted alongside the importance of carers. This view of ethics fits well not only with a relational view of competence described in the last chapter, but also with Young's (2000) view of democracy which highlights that, since relationships create ambiguity, differences in communicative style need to be embraced by participatory work. Children's varying symbolic use of the 'Who Chooses' activity is, thus, seen as difference, rather than deficit, though it is suggested that it generally pointed to their need for regard from others.

Thus, it is argued, children's friendships in the classroom are in the early stages and are based on individual and shared pleasure. Dunn and Brown (2001) also reinforce that observation of these friendships demonstrates that children possess continuity in social understanding which may not be evident in psychological tests. Importantly, by allowing opportunities for family life to be vocalised in the classroom, the teacher can have an important role in guiding children's emotional understanding and can actively help children to build new friendships. Nevertheless, the authority of the teacher to influence children in this way rests on the way that authority is viewed by young children in the classroom. Thus it is the children's question: 'Who's in charge?' that we consider in the next chapter.

Chapter 7

Who's in charge?

Doing as you're told?

In this chapter, the power relationship between adults and children in the classroom is discussed as well as the less accessible area of leadership and power amongst the children themselves. In the same way that competence was discussed, less from an individual and more from a relational theoretical viewpoint, so too leadership, with its connotations of power and authority, is looked at from the viewpoint of social practices. This draws on the Foucauldian (1982) notion that identity is both deeply social and created by and inseparable from power. Therefore, the theoretical perspective of the chapter challenges an exclusively individual view of a leader as someone particularly visionary or personally charismatic.

Devine (2000) also discusses power relations between adults and children in school from a Foucauldian perspective. Her view is that 'teacher power and control within the classroom is never complete' (p.190) since children are always mediating and adapting the adult definitions of the appropriate norms for them. Thus, whilst teachers in a classroom provide a form of leadership and control, it can never be absolute since the dynamics of peer relations must be considered. Devine found, in her research in Irish schools, that children gained control over their school lives through an autonomous culture constructed through both overt and covert resistances. These findings help to inform the findings in the project, in that whilst, to different degrees, children sought out adult authority, they also demonstrated the need to seek out power structures within their peer group. In this way they were discovering who was in charge in the classroom and how best to relate to that.

The issue of power and leadership in the classroom, from the child's perspective, is difficult to gain access to by interview because children will often tailor their responses on this subject particularly closely to their perceived expectations of the adult questioner. This reinforces the power exercised by adults when they use spoken language to communicate. The children at Allen Road seemed particularly aware of adult authority. They tended to search my face for the appropriate answer to questions and used words which adults approved of, such as 'wait, say please' and 'share'. Their strategies for gaining longer turns on the bikes showed a genius for harnessing adult approval for their own ends, such as putting on a paramedic coat to make the bike into an ambulance (the outdoor theme) or saying they'd just 'got here', a key factor in adult rationale for turn-taking. When asked how they would deal with a play situation in which 'someone else came and said "I want that"', most children replied 'I'd tell the teacher.' Tom seemed especially keen to gain recognition through adult approval. Asked whether he liked it best when he chose or when someone else told him what to do, he said that he liked it when someone told him what to do. He often repeated the answer that was suggested by the adult.

Nevertheless, the Allen Road teacher's circle time routine every morning enabled the children to initiate talk about their experiences and listen to each other, often talking at length about getting hurt and being brave. This practice seemed to shape a sense of mutual experience which didn't rely solely on the teacher and thus developed children's competence to share decision-making in the classroom with the adults. This constructed children, as suggested in chapter four, as 'members' of a relatively small class of 18–20 children and this membership counteracted their tendencies otherwise to comply with authority without question.

The children at St Bede's appeared to strive, more than the other classes, to find authority from within their own ranks. This was the biggest class of the three which served an upwardly mobile, semi-rural social area. Indeed, one could argue that the children reflected competitiveness in their behaviour because of the value of space, in this context, both inside and outside the classroom, making the battle for recognition more intense. Andrew's comment, previously discussed in chapter five: 'When I grow up I think I'll buy this school' can also be related to Devine's (2000, p.194) research suggesting that symbolic power between adults and children is expressed by the fact that 51 per cent of the children thought that the teachers 'owned the school'. In this light, Andrew recognised, more than other children in the class, that the struggle for influence amongst peer group is surpassed by the authority of the adults and that ownership in the adult world is the real way to secure space and, therefore, power. Confidence to speak his mind to adults also reflected his understanding that communication gave him access to leadership.

Children at Cooper Street accepted the authority of the adults in their classroom and, with the exception of David, seemed less competitive. They sought adult help to solve their disputes and even to arbitrate turn-taking on the seesaw outside. Even when David was asked about what he would do to access a turn on equipment that another child was playing with, he knew that he was supposed to ask first. He replied that he would say: 'Can I have what you're playing with please?' However, he also quickly added: '… and tell the teacher on them if they won't let me have a go.' David was really only happy to share if he was in charge, but sometimes other children rejected his authority and turned to the teacher to sort him out instead. His response was to gain authority from adults by telling them about other children's misdemeanours as often as possible; for example, after one playtime he told me that Annie had pushed him and that Lenny's chewing gum wasn't allowed. This competitiveness was also evident in another example when he was playing with the bricks with Lenny, during which the play developed into a competition to make the longest structure from a line of bricks. This task drove the play for a while until eventually David realised that amassing the biggest pile of bricks was the key to making the longest structure and therefore this became his aim. This again demonstrated that David knew and utilised the language of winning.

The teacher at Cooper Street used organisational tools such as rotas to enable the children to take turns in setting out the outdoor play equipment. In this way, the children were conceived of as 'helpers' whilst the adults retained control of the situation. David related well to this system, as, like Andrew at St Bede's, he understood that adults needed to be negotiated with in order to access a leadership position amongst one's peers. Children at Cooper Street generally did not utilise the rules for sharing that they had been taught without recourse to an adult. When their teacher introduced a timer as a way for the children to organise turn-taking without her intervention she commented that it was 'like getting blood out of a stone' trying to get them to recognise this as a solution to the issue of sharing.

Nevertheless, Cooper Street's was the class in which the children seemed most harmonious and able to play together without conflict. They seemed to have made friendships, despite a context where the teacher was overtly in charge of the situation. This contrasted with the teaching style at St Bede's, in which, although the teacher's power and control was mediated by a focus on the children's communication skills, nevertheless, conflicts were frequent. This suggests that retaining teacher control does not necessarily diminish the level of children's co-operation or, vice versa, relinquishing control does not improve it. However, the situation at Allen Road perhaps struck the most useful balance of power through the teacher's concentration on the children's emotional development. In this way, the teacher's authority was directed towards developing the children's competence to relate to each other through becoming confident individuals, an important foundation for the communication and co-operation aimed at in the other classes. Without the emotional security of circle time, I would suggest that Cooper Street children, despite some harmony, were not building independent co-operation for the future and St Bede's children were potentially overwhelmed by too many intellectual demands and significantly higher class numbers.

Making decisions

Devine (2000) points out that individuals exercise as well as undergo power. Thus children 'position themselves in the light of the expectations and evaluations of significant other' (p.190). This suggests, as has been shown, that the children in all three classes were all able to exercise power as relevant to that context, a factor which David in particular was well aware of. However, Devine also notes that the younger children in her study accepted the authority of adults relatively unquestioningly, a finding which is also supported by this study in that no children directly challenged the teacher's right to control the class. Nevertheless, it was an aim of this study that the children should be introduced to, and made aware of, decision-making processes in their lives, in order to demonstrate that adults might not always be the only arbiters of power. This awareness was initiated through the 'Who Chooses' activity described in chapter six. However, it was also an aim that children were introduced to decision-making in a collective context in the classroom, as well as in their individual lives. The first activity which aimed at raising this type of awareness was the voting activity (see p.92) which, by using symbols to externalise the individual's role in decision-making, was designed to be a practical demonstration of the concept of agency.

The method used for voting in the classroom was polling, as opposed to casting ballots. This meant that the children made their choices in public and the outcomes were also acted on in public, making the adults accountable both for the outcome and the process of voting. Votes were cast as a means of collective decision-making about class activities, such as which stories were read and whether certain games were played. Interestingly, the public nature of the decision-making did not seem to affect the decisions made as much as one might have expected and changing of minds during the voting process seemed more to do with further reflection than peer group influence.

Voting is part of a style of democracy which does not necessarily embrace Young's (2000) participatory politics, which involves recognition of difference rather than decision made by a majority. Nevertheless, a system in which each person has one vote, and the majority wins, has the appeal of simplicity and transparency, making communication with a diverse audience, including children, easier. De Vries and Zan (1994) go further to suggest that voting is an important part 'of the socio-moral atmosphere of the constructivist classroom' (p.145). They claim that voting can give children an opportunity 'to construct the idea of equality' through the equal weight given to each person's vote in the decision-making process. Certainly the ownership of an object or token with which to cast a vote did seem to give the children in all three classes a strong sense of their own part in the final decision. It was also hoped that the activity would stimulate some children to question a majority decision, thus opening up consideration of minority viewpoints and a more participatory outlook.

Allen Road was the first class who was invited to vote. The issue was whether they preferred indoor or outdoor play. This was a decision with no immediate consequences or action, so was regarded by the adults as a pilot attempt at testing the voting procedure. The children were given a conker to hold while they considered the issue. It was noticeable to all the adults present that holding an object seemed to focus the children's attention to the question in such a way that they appeared less concerned with giving 'the right answer' – a tendency of this class – and more concerned with independent thinking. Importantly, the class teacher and nursery nurse also voted (though last), illustrating a parity of adult with child influence about the issue. Whilst considering their response, the children sat in a circle and as each cast their vote there was a sense of individuals relating to a group structure.

Whereas De Vries and Zan (1994) make a case for the practice of voting to connect with the practice of equality, this does not necessarily mean that the needs of the minority are catered for. As mentioned earlier, I had hoped that voting itself would prompt children to question the position of the children who had 'lost' the vote. De Vries and Zan also say that 'through exchanging points of view, children may be persuaded to make new efforts to persuade others' (p.145) which suggests that voting can stimulate debate itself. My findings, instead, point to children's acceptance of the right of the majority over the minority. Indeed, at Allen Road, the system of voting proved so popular that the teacher observed children adopting voting in their play to help solve arguments about what to do. In this way, majority rule was unquestioned and, rather than stimulating further debate, actually served to extinguish it.

This tendency at Allen Road was not as accentuated in the other two classes. Although the children in the other classes were similarly solemn about the process of voting, there were no observed instances of them using voting in their own play. Learning from the experiences at Allen Road, the teacher at St Bede's decided to use her problem-solving approach with the children to question them after votes were counted about how the children who had lost the vote might feel. Amy said that they would feel sad and this enabled the teacher to ask the children: 'What can we do to help the children who feel sad?' This prompted Clare to say that the children who had lost the vote 'should have a turn to choose tomorrow'. In this way, children were introduced to a more multi-dimensional concept of fairness than that of majority rule.

The attractiveness of young children making decisions by voting was arguably that of providing clarity of purpose without reliance on verbal skills. However, in terms of enabling participation, the use of voting as a technique proved to have limited value, its very concreteness suggesting to the children that decisions were fixed. Whilst this had the attractiveness of certainty, it tended to limit rather than raise questions and thereby stifled, rather than stimulated, debate.

However, another method which was used with the children to enable collective decision-making involved dramatising conflict and possible solutions through reading the class a story. In this method, the use of narrative provided the children with a context for debate which they could then relate to their own situations. At Cooper Street, a story called *Herbert and Harry* (Allen, 1990) was read to the whole class which related to a competition between two brothers to get rich, fuelled by mutual suspicion. This plot was then related to the play situation, previously recounted, between David and Lenny, in which the common goal to build became obscured by the desire of each individual to acquire more bricks. In this way, the initial narrative of the story provided a template for thinking and debating issues of fairness which otherwise seemed an elusive topic for class, or indeed individual, discussion. The concept and practice of fairness here seemed to be dominated by either adult pressure or self-interest. Similarly, at Allen Road, Jake thought that he should have a turn on the computer straight away rather than waiting behind someone else who had been waiting longer than he had. This class seemed to vacillate between '*sharing*' (adult-speak) or '*grabbing*' (child-tactic).

The story of *Playing Together* (see p.91) was conceived following the success in all the classes of using stories for promoting listening and discussion. The story recounts the decisions, difficulties and conflicts which two children, in this case boys, face when they opt to play together. The absence of adults means that they have to find solutions on their own if they want the play to continue. The premise of creating this story was the opportunity it gave for children to intervene and play a part in its telling. This involved the recognition that listening can play a significant part, not only in the individual interpretation of meanings but also in collective ones. This additional feature was designed to enable the children to share ideas and, indeed, participate within the security of an accessible narrative framework.

At this point in the project, the Cooper Street class had to withdraw (due to a change of teacher), so the story was only read to children at Allen Road and St Bede's. Not surprisingly, given their previous experience of voting, the children in both the remaining classes offered solutions to the dilemma of the children in the story which included suggestions such as: 'they could vote' and 'they could work as a team'. Alternatively they suggested that: 'first they played at his house and then tomorrow they go to the other house' or 'they could decide that both of them want to do something that's the same'. Taking turns was suggested and also the possibility that they could play football, an idea not included in the story but which was prompted by the football which one of the pictured 'story' children was carrying.

Perhaps less in the spirit of co-operation, some children suggested that one of the children in the story should give way to the other or that they could each go their separate ways to do as they wished. At Allen Road, a question resolving the argument about who should build the den in the story was repeatedly answered by gestures to demonstrate how the den should be built. Whilst it was tempting to think that the children had failed to understand the complexity of my question and also lacked the verbal skills to answer it, an alternative explanation, offered by a support teacher colleague, was that the children were in fact telling me how the argument would be resolved through activity or 'just getting on with it'. This, arguably, mirrors not just children's, but also adults' ways of resolving many disputes.

In this pragmatic vein, the children listening also became unexpectedly concerned with the issues in the story presented by sharing a bottle of juice without cups and the number of blankets needed for building two dens. Thus, one child in St Bede's pointed out: 'there won't be enough blankets' and children in each class pointed out that cups were missing from the story and that two children drinking out of one bottle was problematic.

These examples of child-initiated concern suggest that the children listening to the story were aware of the complexity of sharing, particularly when adults are not around to provide a leadership and decision-making function. However, the issues raised by the children also revealed a contextual concern with practicality which suggested that this was the basis for their exercise of power and recognition of leadership, rather than the proficiency with language and argument which characterise more adult tools. Put more succinctly, Donaldson (1978) says that children can show 'skill as thinkers and language users to a degree... as long as they are dealing with 'real-life' meaningful situations in which they have purposes and intentions'. In other words, their level of language skill is embedded in the situation rather than abstracted from it.

'You're not coming to my party'

In the St Bede's reception class, as previously suggested, many of the children seemed to think that they were already in charge. A classroom assistant commented that the children were both more 'unruly' than last year as well as more 'confident'. Although their recourse to adult authority was not as noticeable as in the other two classes, their relationships could seem quite harsh. The 'Co-operative Faces' game revealed paired rivalries and children vying with each other to achieve influence. In this environment, the demands to achieve authority within the peer group rested strongly on children's ability to make friends. Abi's status in the class was, thus, seen by other children as low in this respect. However, her range of possible friends was also limited because peer relationships in the classroom environment were likely to be made with children with perceived parallel levels of development and in this respect, Abi was an individual in the class.

Nevertheless, the teacher at St Bede's worked hard to communicate strategies to the children to enable them to work more successfully together. She frequently wrote down their constructive ideas, such as: 'if we all go and get milk together we get squashed' and these ideas were read back to them. The children were also encouraged to enact stories and suggest solutions to each other's distress. A collision was re-enacted at group time with the question: 'what could we do?' Gradually the children began to consider these types of problems more carefully and the expected answers of 'say sorry' and 'walk' gave way to more thoughtful suggestions. In this way, the teacher relied on communication and narratives to enable to children to co-construct their environment. However, despite these efforts, it was consistently most obvious at St Bede's that the children were using not just practical skills but also a social currency of party invitations to gain position. As we saw in chapter six, Abi had learnt quickly that saying 'You're not coming to my party' was an effective defence when she was criticised by other girls. But parties were not just the concern of girls, their social currency suggested leadership and power amongst boys, too. For instance when Freddie was telling me about a Halloween party, the conversation naturally led onto his friendships and he confided to me that he played with 'no one' in the classroom. I then asked him who he wanted to play with and he named a child who was playing with a group of boys around the train track. When I asked the named child if Freddie could play he said he would have to ask one of the others in the group.

In this way, access to play, as well as to parties, was clearly regulated by particular 'successful' individuals to whom the other children deferred decisions about who else could join in the play. On this occasion, Freddie, a shy and reserved boy, was allowed into the play; perhaps because of my involvement in, and deferral to, the process of recognising this hierarchy of social competence. Corsaro (2005, p.141) suggests that the defensiveness of a play situation by an existing group or pair of children signifies an intense involvement 'in creating a sense of sharing during the actual course of playing together'. Thus the hierarchy would refer to who was involved in the original development of the play. The difficulty for children such as Freddie was that he was not likely to be an instigator of play and, therefore, he was constantly trying to gain entry to play and being resisted by other children. Although this seems harsh, Corsaro suggests that over time, most children 'develop a complex set of access strategies' (p.141) to counteract this difficulty. Thus, my negotiation may have been a very temporary measure to Freddie's exclusion. Perhaps, in the light of this example, the voting in play adopted by Allen Road children, as described earlier, is a startling attempt at a more democratic concept of leadership.

It seems appropriate here to give the teachers a voice on their own perception of authority in the classroom. The teachers were asked at the end of the first term about the impact of the project on their practice. All three teachers commented that the project had raised their awareness about their own role in the classroom in relation to children's decision-making. St Bede's teacher also commented that she had reflected on 'the balance of power' in the classroom and how children could be given a voice. The Cooper Street teacher felt that young children were able 'to be independent and make decisions on a much higher level' than she had previously realised. The Allen Road teacher cited herself as 'becoming a partner' with the children in decision-making and, of the three, was in the best position to utilise the project as a means to changing her role in the classroom. She attributed this partly to the change of leadership in her school which had led to an emphasis on the early years provision and also to having far fewer children in the reception class than in the previous year. This emphasised that leadership beyond the classroom clearly impacted on what went on within it, a point that bears appropriate reassertion in this chapter.

The Allen Road teacher also continued to find the project beneficial as a catalyst in developing her practice. At the end of the project she reported her amazement at how self-motivating and responsible for their own learning the children had become. This she attributed to the children being given choices and having their views treated as 'relevant and important'. Choice-making for this group, in her view, was linked to 'responding in a responsible and mature way' as well as 'accepting the views of others'. The teacher at St Bede's was less unequivocal at the end of the project but felt that she wanted to 'know more and read more about listening to children'. She felt that reflection on practice was the main benefit of being involved in the project. For her, a good story often left 'a question hanging in the air'.

Summary

In this chapter, I have used notions of power and leadership as interrelated terms. A Foucauldian approach to power (1982), reflected also in the work of Devine (2000), has provided an understanding of leadership which is more obscure to the adult eye than might be expected. Leadership amongst children dwells in the terrain of a secret society and though adults can often discern which children lack this quality, it is not always easy to see which children retain it. At St Bede's, party invitations were observed as the currency of this authority between children. Nevertheless, the exercise of adult power in all the classrooms was clearly accepted as the norm by children and, indeed, mediating this power, by delegating it to the children, created at least a temporary sense of unease.

The practice of voting has been discussed as a structure which replaces adult authority with a different kind of authority: that of the majority. The children at Allen Road found that this authority was a significant factor in determining their disputes away from their teacher. She, meanwhile, retained another kind of authority through attention to the children's understanding of emotional issues. Further investigation of authority in the classroom also suggests that the leadership style of the adult may be inversely related to the leadership style amongst the children. It seemed that the more that authority was delegated to the children's ability to solve their own problems, the more power became distributed amongst fewer children and where adult authority was clearly asserted, the children deferred to it, rather than to each other. This confirmed the importance of the teacher as a leader in the classroom and thus the style of leadership as of immense pedagogical significance.

The findings of this chapter, therefore, point to a model of participation at the start of school that has to be mediated through adult authority and attention to children's (as indeed all humans') need for security and consistency. Leadership in the reception classroom has to concentrate on providing a structure that will support an understanding of the power of decision-making, both individually and collectively. However, many decisions will be made by the adult to support the rights of the minority. In this way, a role model is provided for the exercise of participatory democracy which children can adopt through the more sophisticated structures of debate which they can access better when they are older.

In terms of participatory methods which children can work with in the present, the use of narratives, as demonstrated in the example of the children's responses to the *Playing Together* story, has been shown as more effective than voting. This provided a format for structuring decision-making to support debate and enable young children to consider multiple viewpoints. Thus, by stimulating imagination, narrative was seen to both open up the exercise of leadership to a wider audience and also help the audience to grasp each other's perspectives. Nevertheless, as already indicated, the ability to understand other perspectives is a lifelong aim which young children are, at best, only embarking upon. Thus, it is important that once new alliances have begun to form in the classroom, the teacher concentrates on her or his role as rule maker, as well as leader. It is this aspect of classroom life which is examined in the next chapter. This is the aspect of boundaries and common value which prompts the children to question: 'What am I allowed to do?'

Chapter 8

What am I allowed to do?

Routines and rituals

This final chapter examines the questions which concern young children starting school, it will consider how children ascertain what behaviour is expected of them in the classroom. This relates directly to the issue of (in)equality and (re)distribution of resources, for which the previous three chapters have set the scene. It covers two important aspects of rules: the covert and the overt. 'Covert' rules, it is suggested, are the routines and rituals of the classroom environment which govern children as much, if not more than, they are governed by more formal 'overt' rules. In using the word 'covert' to describe routines, it is not implied that these are necessarily negative, merely that they often function with less critical scrutiny, and indeed sometimes more effectiveness, than other forms of governance. Thus, they need careful appraisal to evaluate how, if at all, they contribute to children's participation in the classroom.

We have already seen, with reference to Bruner's 'epiphanies of the ordinary' (1983) that it is not just familiar people but also familiar routines in children's daily lives that provide the format for transmitting language and culture (Dunn and Brown, 2001). Jackson (1982) found that the organisation and routines of the reception class were crucial in enabling children to settle in to the new environment. This view of the settling process is supported by the notion of 'habitus' which Bourdieu (1990) conceptualises as a mechanism which makes sense of a new environment by enabling people to utilise dispositions which have been built on familiar knowledge. Brooker's (2002) fairly recent study of children starting school directly alludes to this idea of 'habitus' to explain how children from a diversity of family backgrounds make the transition into the culture of school. Clearly, in some cases, a mismatch between the routines and values that constitute the familiar knowledge of home and school means that 'family habitus' constrains a child from making the transition to school smoothly.

It is possible, through Brooker's (2002) work, to understand how children's family backgrounds influence their ability to settle in to the reception class setting and the stories of Tom and David support this in different ways. However, this project focused on how teachers' practice in the making of a 'classroom habitus' can help to bridge these divides between home and school which many children experience. This rests on the teacher's ability to provide the children with a sense of security, in terms of the routines and rituals of class life, which allows rules to be understood and benefit all. This is an aim which implies that participation in a classroom environment requires a level of structure and repetition to allow children to settle as individuals and cohere as a group. Thus, the process of 'settling in' is dependent not just on family, but also on teaching practices, as we have seen in the example of children's emotional development in circle time in the class at Allen Road.

The theme of rules, of all those identified, arguably relied the most on the teacher. Although children clearly desired the fairness and commonality of rules, they looked to the teacher for assistance with upholding them. The examples given from Allen Road, in particular, point to a deep ambivalence with children's implementation of rules for sharing when left to their own devices. As discussed in chapter five, this was partly due to the hesitancy of these children's verbal communication, but it was also to do with the impracticality and lack of clarity of the rules themselves.

For instance, when children were asked what they would do if they wanted a turn on a bike, the reply was generally: 'wait'. There was no answer to the following question: 'Do you ever go and say, "I want a turn?" They suggested that they would 'say please' in order to 'get' a turn and only Tom admitted that really he would 'go up and grab it!' However since Tom was acutely aware of the need for adult authority, he also agreed that adults provided useful guidance about play: 'This is good, isn't it – play a bit wi' that, a bit wi' that.' He was also keen to show his awareness of the adult rule that only two children are allowed in the home corner at one time, even if at times he didn't stick to it. On the whole, therefore, children demonstrated confusion about rules and when asked about what the rules were, they vacillated between saying: 'you let people have a go' and 'you tell the teacher'. They seemed to be stuck due to a discrepancy between theory and practice which meant that they had to defer to adult authority to sort out disputes.

The children at St Bede's, who were generally more assertive than the children at Allen Road, were less uneasy about the potential contradictions of negotiating adult rules. Carrie told me that she made the rules and when asked again said that she made the rules with the teacher. A group of children who were playing together insisted 'the children make the rules' and when two children were asked about whose idea it was to use a timer to regulate turn-taking on the computer, they said that it was their idea. This confidence could also be attributed to the skill of their teacher who used visual aids, puppets and toys to 'tell' the children about routines and rules. She demonstrated rules clearly, by aids such as a zigzag line on the floor against which children could line up. Incidents where children had been hurt were reported back to the children as stories which needed happier endings. Alongside this deferral to the children she also exerted her own authority when necessary, by stating: 'I'm not listening because I've started the story.' In this way, children were invited to co-construct the environment within stated boundaries which included teacher authority. However, despite the boundary, the atmosphere was often one of struggle between the most confident children. This could be attributed to the size of this class, which at near to thirty was the largest and busiest of the three. This provided a challenge since the teacher's invitation to the children to co-construct the environment shifted a responsibility onto them which arguably needed more support than one adult could provide to this size of group.

In the smaller class at Cooper Street, children were well versed in knowing the rules but, as previously discussed, they relied on adults to enforce them. When Jake was asked to share the hedgehog he was playing with, Lenny informed me, 'First you ask for a turn and then you fetch an adult.' Charley, expecting additional complications, explained that: 'If they don't give it me and if they hit you, I tell the teacher' and not surprisingly, David took it upon himself to report to adults when he saw something happening that was 'against the rules'. In practice, without an adult to arbitrate the entire process, grabbing what they wanted sometimes provided the best way forward for these children. It seemed, therefore, that despite a classroom environment in which children generally exerted high levels of competence, their ability to implement common regulations frequently foundered. Thus, in all three classes, the issue of rules created ambiguity and potential confusion for the children.

This situation provides a good argument that we should engage children more rigorously in the process of rule-making and set up systems for doing so. Nixon (2001, p.232) suggests that, since participation is about fair debate, the nature of the debate is as important as its outcome. The Habermasian (1984; 1987) approach to debate, which emphasises consensus, also outlines that the provision of a form of justice should be determined by the participants. These views suggest that children engaged in a participatory process of rule-making will, in so doing, become subjected to rules of fairness which stem from the recognition of others. In this way, it is proposed that the gap between the theory and practice of social justice should begin to lessen. Nevertheless, the structure for achieving this approach also needs initiation and the input of a leader. Although the children in the project demonstrated emotional and social competence, the cognitive and arguably 'rational' demands of debate remained elusive. Though this need not be characterised as a weakness, it demonstrates that the structures for rule-making often remain in the adult domain.

This acknowledgement of the rationale needed to provide structures for rule-making relates well to Bauman's (2002) reservations about the politics of recognition succeeding the politics of redistribution. Bauman stresses that the politics of recognition must be firmly attached to notions of social justice or difference 'may have to be paid for with distributive handicap in the competitive game of resources and rewards' (p.144). This means that even relating well to each other socially and emotionally may not, on its own, be enough to guarantee fairness in the classroom. At Allen Road, this was the situation. However, the children who were growing in emotional awareness did, at least, seem to be growing aware of the inconsistency of the rules, even if they were not yet able to resolve the inconsistency collectively.

Bending and unbending the rules

Devine (2000) suggests that children's participation is meaningless unless it occurs at a systemic and organisational level and thus we could argue that the rule-making in the Allen Road and Cooper Street classes foundered because it fell short of this level of participation. However, the more progressive practice at St Bede's, where children were involved in co-constructing class rules, suggested that a teacher *giving* children responsibility to make rules was also not necessarily the way for children to *experience* the responsibility of rule-making. Devine (2000) helps us to understand this by highlighting the importance of children's own relationships as necessary motivational factors in the struggle for democracy at all levels. In this respect, the children at St Bede's were still in the early stages of forming peer relationships in the classroom. Devine also identifies that children have ingenious ways of adapting adult rules to comply with their own interests. For example, in order to avoid giving up a bike to another child, Alan, at Allen Road, said that he had 'just got here' which linked to the rule that a certain amount of time was allowed for each turn. As recounted on page 72, Shane told me that his bike was 'an ambulance' as he knew that the teacher had introduced the hospital theme into the outdoor play area by making paramedic jackets available to wear.

Observations like these suggest that, though children often find adult rules impenetrable and irrelevant to their situation, they sometimes experience rule-making themselves by 'playing for time' and applying versions of rules to get the best result, all the more so when they have secure peer relationships. Their recitation of adult rules reveals that although they know what they are supposed to say, they find what is feasible to be different.

However, children bending rules should not be seen as a way to increase pupil participation, even if it allows them to adapt to inconsistent situations. Involving children in the process of rule-making not only has educational potential, as discussed earlier and pointed out by Nixon *et al.* (1996), but also enables a class to function more cohesively (Osler, 2000). Thus, Davies and Kirkpatrick's (2000) research suggests that fewer discipline problems are found in European schools, even in socially deprived areas, than in UK schools because of higher levels of pupil participation. However, pupil participation at a systemic level, as Kirby *et al.* (2003) contend, is hard to find anywhere. Even the work of the United Nations on children's rights, though identifying injustices, has so far failed to involve children at a systemic level in the finding of solutions. Skrtic (1991), discussing school systems, suggests that this problem lies in the different forms of rationality implied by bureaucracy and democracy. When schools adopt a predominantly bureaucratic form of organisation, the participation of children inherent in the practice of democratic ideals is constrained. As was noted in chapter two, Skrtic (1991, p.184) proposes that schools should become 'adhocratic', a system that would allow children to influence their course.

An adhocatic system, which we suggested in chapter three as particularly fitting for early years practices, would involve young children in a reception class in rule-making and, thereby, it would encourage the difficult concept of 'waiting for a turn' (Cuffaro, 1995). This implies that children's participation in rule-making is primarily a tool for their learning and knowledge-construction (De Vries and Zan, 1994). However, the teacher at St Bede's, previously characterised as the teacher most committed to inviting children's participation in rule-making, also struggled with making this process successful. When she asked her class: 'What makes our class a smiley place to be?' the children answered with the suggestions they had heard before, either at home or school, such as: 'when we are helpful and kind; when we are gentle'. Furthermore, the children appeared unsettled in this classroom and I would contend that they often found this level of co-construction of rules bewildering unless the parameters were consistently reinforced. It is, therefore, difficult to avoid the implication, as discussed earlier in this chapter in relation to the implementation of Habermas's ideas, that children settling into school together do need some level of guidance about their social behaviour, with known consequences if it becomes anti-social.

For children such as Abi, at St Bede's, who found belonging and conforming to a group difficult, adult guidance was only effective when tailored towards her as an individual. She was often unwilling to sit and listen with the whole class group without causing a disturbance by moving or making noises. Although this was most noticeable in Abi's behaviour when the class were together, nevertheless, the size of the class and design of the classroom also meant that two or three other children found the demands of sitting and listening difficult and this is by no means unusual in a reception class setting.

De Vries and Zan (1994) discuss how rules may be applied to young children in these situations. They point out that, because the young child 'cannot think beyond surface observables, the spirit of many rules is unknowable' (p.30). This means that the journey towards co-operative behaviour and self-regulation is a gradual one which requires the teacher to encourage the child using a respectful mixture of coercion and co-operation. This is an educative process which can be viewed as cognitive, in terms of a development of theory of mind, and also emotional, as was prioritised in the practice of the teacher at Allen Road. In Abi's case, the mixture needed may have differed from that needed by the majority of children in the class, so learning in a smaller group could have been more successful to ensure the correct conditions for her moral growth in terms of interpersonal issues. As previously stated, this requirement is not easy to satisfy in a class which is often staffed by just one adult.

Nevertheless, there is also evidence in the project that the difficulty of educating a large class of young children, who may be at different stages in the development of their moral reasoning towards self-regulation, can be made smoother with the utilisation of familiar routines and patterns, previously discussed in this chapter and identified as the classroom 'habitus' (Bourdieu, 1990). An example of this occurred in the class at St Bede's where the 'Who Chooses' activity revealed the children's desire for pattern, as demonstrated by their interest in the exactness of the number, the colour of the stickers and the spontaneous subtraction activities which this led to. These patterns seemed to help the children consider the questions, much as the holding of a token had helped them to reflect before voting, and it appeared that ritualising an activity was an important aid for considering issues of participation.

At Allen Road and Cooper Street, it was possible to identify this phenomenon with the repetition of the questions, which caused children to engage in pre-empting the next question and rote-counting the stickers. At Allen Road, even the pattern of the stickers on the page was commented on with: 'I got some funny eyes.' At Cooper Street, the children began to make patterns with their stickers as they placed them and the rhythm of the questioning started to determine a corresponding pattern of answers by the group, with the answer 'me!' becoming more prevalent.

Thus, despite critique in this book of De Vries and Zan's (1994) developmental explanations for children's different levels of self-regulation, nevertheless, I agree with them that it is the practices of the teacher in creating a coherent and secure environment for children within a 'constructivist' framework that 'optimally' (p.3) promote their playfulness and development. De Vries and Zan emphasise in their approach to 'the development of a science of educational practice' (p.3) a co-operative approach to teaching that can engender 'active thoughtfulness about reasons for rules' (p.51). Thus it is suggested that the teacher should ask rather than tell, and persuade rather than control. These are the tactics that avoid power struggles and allow children the possibility of becoming self-regulating participants in the classroom.

The pattern of narrative

The last section suggested that both coherence of routine and persuasive language are important for young children's understanding of rules. With this in mind, it is possible to see that narrative structure can also provide children with a mediation between being told and being asked as well as 'an active orientation to ideas of self and others' (De Vries and Zan, 1994, p.51).

The creation and use of the story *Playing Together* was intended to have just such an effect. Through its simple and repetitive structure the story provided the necessary routine and predictability combined with opportunities for children to engage intellectually with the process of rule-making. As previously discussed, this activity allowed children to express interpretations of fairness in a way that other methods had failed at. Whereas formerly children had recited rules when asked about achieving fairness, it was evident in the responses to this story that it produced a higher level of engagement with issues of conflict resolution and rule-making. In some cases, children used the pattern of the narrative as a structure to add new ideas onto the existing story. Thus Sam said 'Charlie said: "Let's go for a walk" and Harry agreed.' Thereby, children felt supported in thinking about the realities of applying social rules rather than relying on the token gestures of 'waiting for a turn' and 'sharing', which they claimed to apply to their own class situation, but with little evidence of success.

The responses to *Playing Together* also revealed the practical concerns of the children with regard to making rules. Whilst engaging in a discussion about how the children in the story could share the juice, Tom said 'you'd have to cup your hands'. Similarly, at St Bede's, children were concerned that 'you're not allowed to drink out of one bottle' and also in another part of the story that 'there wouldn't be enough blankets'. It is possible to apply a developmental approach to illuminate these comments. De Vries and Zan (1994, p.34) refer to Selman's (1980) 'levels of enacted interpersonal understanding' as a provisional framework for identifying children's social development. Adopting this, these examples would suggest that children are operating at what is called a 'reciprocal reflective level' which highlights that they were sharing experience through joint reflection on similar perceptions or experiences. In Selman's scheme, this comes at level two and follows level one which is the 'unilateral one-way level' and level nought, which is the 'egocentric impulsive level'. At level two, negotiation occurs through co-operative strategies and is succeeded by the 'mutual third-person level' at level three.

Certainly, with reference to the examples above, using the *Playing Together* story with children in the project resulted in an orientation of their comments away from the adult storyteller and towards each other, which was one of the aims of using narrative as a research method. In addition to the developmental framework used above to explain children's comments, the practicality of their thinking could also be characterised as an aspect of the concept of 'praxis' (Freire, 1970), in that their view of knowledge linked with actual experiences and thus made it more meaningful and motivating as a topic for discussion.

Whichever explanation of children's comments is used, it seems that narrative often provided the most significant moments in supporting children to become 'autonomous and critical learners' (Young, 2000, p.118). Whether, as De Vries and Zan (1994) suggest, coercion can accompany co-operation in the path to achieving this aim must be a subject of continued debate. Young's (2000) approach to participation suggests against this, since she says that autonomy is only attained through participation by forming 'validity judgements in actual social situations of unequal power and authority' (p.121). However, the study which focused on young children suggests that adult-led routines and rituals in the classroom, which might be viewed as coercive, do have a significant role to play in building children's confidence and sense of security in a new environment. Furthermore, this study also suggests that narrative patterns have a vital role in providing a bridge between this sense of security and the beginnings of debate. This then engages children in interpersonal interactions which involve the creation of rules. Unless children become involved in this way, the evidence of the project showed that, even in the most sympathetic classrooms, they will continue to rely on adults to enforce rules which are beyond their ability to implement. In this way the path between coercion and co-operation will become blocked.

Although the teachers at both Allen Road and Cooper Street discussed giving children more opportunities to resolve conflicts themselves, it was the teacher at St Bede's who specifically identified that her children needed 'to make the classroom rules with the adults' which also involved 'clear consequences'. The teacher at Allen Road found that, by the end of the project, children were able to discuss 'suitable punishments for various offences' which was presented as an example of these children's growing tendency to contribute ideas about a number of aspects of classroom life. It has been discussed that attention to the emotional aspects of relationship building, as demonstrated in the practices of this teacher, can support the foundations of rule-making; nevertheless, in the busier class at St Bede's, this level of support was more difficult to achieve and effective rules became all the more crucial. In this situation, the teacher felt the need for a system with more routine and repetition to support children in observing rules. In the year subsequent to the study, this became one of the priorities and the 'Golden rules' (Mosley and Sonnet, 2005) were introduced.

Summary

This chapter has reinforced points made earlier about the ambiguity of classroom rules in children's eyes which leads to difficulty with their implementation. 'Classroom habitus' has been discussed as a concept which utlises Bourdieu's (1990) concept of 'habitus' and matches Brooker's (2002) notion of 'family habitus'. Since the project sought to identify how participation in a reception class is supported by everyday teaching practices which emphasise routines and rituals, 'classroom habitus' was seen as a focus of the project. It was suggested that this helps children to settle and contribute to discussion.

However, because formal classroom rules often seem tokenistic and leave children to manage as best they can, a strong case is presented for more attempts by teachers to include children in devising rules. Nixon (2001) suggests that by becoming involved in making rules, children will experience principles of social justice and learn to respect these and each other. Nevertheless, the teacher's attempts at St Bede's to help children co-construct classroom rules shows that this practice also needs careful consideration for rules to be enforced, effective and fair for all. This highlights the key issue in this book: that children's individual and relational competence in the classroom needs the overview and leadership of the teacher to ensure fairness and equality in the interim while their social and emotional awareness develop. This is supported in arguments about democracy by Bauman's (2002) reservations about the politics of recognition succeeding (and replacing) the politics of redistribution.

It has also been suggested that children often actually experience rules best when they adapt and use them, in other words, 'bend' them to their own advantage (Devine, 2000). This reinforces that the idea of rules is important to children and that they do engage with them. Thus, involving children in rule-making may involve a mixture of coercion and co-operation to support the children, like Abi, who struggle with the concepts involved (De Vries and Zan, 1994). Rule-making with children presents many pedagogical challenges and can threaten children's sense of security in a busy classroom. However, the project made a strong argument for the use of routines and rituals as supportive to this process.

Finally, in this chapter, narrative method in the form of the story *Playing Together* was presented as effective at enabling children to contribute collectively to rule-making and to understand better a rationale for fair rewards and sanctions in the classroom. Use of narrative in the project stimulated children's practical thinking, demonstrating levels of social awareness which can be understood through both developmental and political frameworks. Thus, narrative is seen as another example of clear patterns in practice which, if it takes account of children's interests and imaginations, can facilitate children's understanding of participation and, therefore, their ability to participate.

I finish this section, however, by reiterating that there will be barriers to children's levels of competence to participate in a reception class with thirty children and one teacher. Although it may be the reality of the reception class as a period of transition to school life, that interim rules have to be exercised by the teacher to establish commonality in the classroom, participatory democracy for children also relies on their emotional growth. In this area I suggest that the leadership of the adult needs to be fairly intimate in order to demonstrate how to take into account a range of perspectives. How this difficult balance in rule-making can be achieved and children's competence as relationship builders can be encouraged in order to establish participatory practice is discussed in the next and final chapter.

Chapter 9

How to plan for participation

Introduction

Transition was one of the themes of the research project described in this book. It was noticeable, as the project progressed, that this theme not only implied a focus on children starting their school lives but also a focus on children as research participants. This meant that the original research questions were superseded by another question which became more important and informed the second of two original questions. This was:

• What does participation mean in a reception class?

Thus, the emphasis of the study moved from existing features of practice and settled instead on the creation of new practices in line with children's own perceptions as research participants. This appeared to increase the importance of the position of parents and peers and decrease the importance of the teacher. However, it was consistent with the theme of participation that this shift of emphasis should occur and that the project itself should be flexible enough in its design to respond to the participants' voices.

Nevertheless, the previous two chapters have also given teachers a central voice in the implementation of participatory aims for children. This is to emphasise that when a group of children are brought together, teaching practices are vital to uphold fairness and the representation of minority views. It is also to emphasise that participation in the classroom is about collective, as well as individual, decision-making and this is an educative, and indeed lifelong, process. The plan for participation, therefore, has to provide opportunities for children and teachers to assert themselves within an overriding principle of recognition of equality and diversity. Whilst it is for teachers to have an overview of these principles, it is for children to develop their innate competence to relate to each other and maintain and bring into the classroom existing loyalties which originate outside of the classroom. Then, in a classroom with participatory teaching practices, they will be encouraged to learn ways to work with perspectives of others in collective decision-making.

The key to achieving these aims for practitioners lies not only in the understanding of the fundamental principles of participation, which have been discussed in chapters two and three, but also in the application of the methods or activities which were outlined in chapter one and which have been described in practice in the subsequent chapters. These, therefore, will first be reiterated in this chapter.

Participatory methods

Co-operative Faces

This game is designed for groups of four children at a time. The task for each individual in the group is to complete a face picture from jigsaw pieces to match a picture they have already been given. However, each child has a mixture of the pieces required for all four pictures. This means that the children need to work together to swap pieces so that each ends up with the pieces to match their own picture.

Taking photos

Children are each invited to take a photo whilst engaged in the normal day-to-day activities. Before the photo is taken each child is asked to try and capture what they like at school. When the photos are printed each child is invited to identify and talk about their photo.

Who Chooses

The 'Who Chooses' activity is used with groups of four children at a time. They are each given a sheet with three outline shapes symbolising themselves, their parents and their teacher. The children are then asked a set of six questions about who makes the decisions about what happens to them in the course of their day. These are:

- Who chooses when you get up in the morning?
- Who chooses what you have for breakfast?
- Who chooses what you do at school?
- Who chooses what you play?
- Who chooses what you watch on TV?
- Who chooses when you go to bed?

The children are asked to respond to the questions by placing a small round sticker in the appropriate shape on their sheet. More shapes are added if children request them.

Voting

Children are each given a token (for example, a conker) and asked to make a choice between two alternatives by placing the token in one of two baskets. Votes are cast as a means of collective decision-making about possible class activities, such as games and stories. The alternative with the most votes is then implemented.

Playing Together

The story *Playing Together* is designed for use with class groups. It recounts the decisions, difficulties and conflicts which two children face when they opt to play together. The absence of adults means that they have to find solutions on their own if they want the play to continue. The story contains several key decisions that the children listening are invited to reflect on and make suggestions for, thus playing a part in the telling and direction of the fictional story. The main teller of the story has to accommodate the suggestions of the listener in shaping alternative directions for the story.

Participatory practices

As well as the application of the methods listed above, which were used to enhance the participatory practices in the project classes, it was important to acknowledge and identify the teaching practices in each class that formed the basis for developing children's participation and sense of belonging. This involved recognising that many of these emanated from existing, and sometimes taken for granted, good practices which were able to accommodate and build on the project methods. Many of these practices relied on allowing the practitioner discretion to exercise their judgement and skill based on theory and experience. Both of these domains as located in practice, rather than primarily in documentation, are, therefore, crucial to participatory teaching practices. Thus, I assert the importance of the teacher, as well as that of the learner, in achieving participatory aims in the classroom.

There were key features of practice identified in each class which encouraged children to be independent of the teacher at points during the day. These varied between the three teachers and for the purposes of the project a particular strength was attributed to each of them (see Table 4.2 on p.44). These strengths corresponded to the three 'c's' of confidence, communication and co-operation (Fountain, 1990) which were seen as fundamental to participation and are also reflected in the key questions heading the chapters in this book. These questions, I contend, inform children's experience of participation at the start of school. Thus, before plans for participation are schematised, I will summarise the key points that ensued from chapters five to eight and relate these to the areas of strength demonstrated by the teachers.

The first key point about reception class practices which the project showed, particularly in the practices of the Allen Road teacher, was that emotional well-being and expression, or 'emotional literacy', was fundamental to decision-making and participation. For children to participate in classroom life, it was vital for them to draw upon their sense of emotional well-being in order to build a foundation of self-confidence, communication and co-operation skills in the new setting. All these attributes are constructed through relationships which children engage in from birth. Without the reciprocation from guardians which builds trust and a sense of security, children will falter in their ability to transfer their skills to a new environment. They will also fail to benefit from a pedagogy that encourages them to make their own decisions.

We saw in the example of Tom that his relatively competent language skills could not compensate for his lack of emotional security. He showed a sense of remorse for his treatment of his brother that suggested an inappropriate sense of responsibility for his young age. Conversely, we saw in David a child with immense self-confidence arising from his understanding of adult concerns. In his case, however, his inclusion into the adult world probably arose because of his status as an only child and therefore familiarity with adult company rather than, as with Tom, premature responsibility being thrust upon him through adult incapability. Whereas David's confidence enabled him to both succeed in formal school skills and act as translator of adult messages to the other children, Tom seemed isolated with his knowledge of the adult world and keen to attract the attention of the adults in the classroom, to the exclusion of other children. Thus, although both David and Tom struggled with peer group relationships, this was only really problematic to Tom.

Abi also struggled with peer group relationships because the other children perceived her inability to communicate and engage in peer group concerns. Nevertheless, there was evidence that Abi was learning these concerns through being in the classroom. Her statement: 'you're not coming to my party' is an effective and apt response to a group of girls criticising her for not helping to tidy up, as is her subsequent declaration that, in fact, 'all the class' were coming to her party. The growth of Abi's confidence during the course of the project was tangible in her gradual ability to maintain a paired friendship in the playground, despite her continued status on the periphery of the class as a whole. Thus we saw, once again, the priority which staking a claim to the new social context takes over proficiency of formal skills of learning. Thus whilst children like Tom, despite competent language, struggled emotionally to build peer relationships and work with other children successfully, children such as Abi, who appeared emotionally secure but lacked expressive language skills, struggled to work with other children without this social competence. This presents a complex picture to a reception teacher, which reinforces the potency of forming positive relationships with parents and carers, and sometimes also taking on the role, as Tom required, of an advocate.

The role of teacher as guide provided the children at Allen Road with lots of opportunities to express their feelings with regard to both home and classroom life. This proved effective in developing these children's ability to relate to each other confidently. Interestingly, however, the Cooper Street teacher's perceived role of tutor also proved effective in teaching some children skills for co-operation. This was mainly boys such as David, for whom these skills were more successfully taught in a didactic way which keyed into their desire to succeed at adult-initiated activities. However, it may be that co-operation skills learnt in this way would not easily transfer to another situation; this merits further study.

The second point which the project suggested was that children's families are crucial to them while they are in the classroom, both in terms of wanting to demonstrate loyalty and love and also as support for making new friends. Since children's ability to form new relationships builds on the recognition and expression of these emotional ties, this area of participatory work was also facilitated most effectively by the practices of the Allen Road teacher, who was also assisted by the intimate atmosphere of a small class size. The awareness-raising activity entitled 'Who Chooses' and the use of photos also provided tools for the children to think with and exercise agency without the immediate burden of responsibility. These were the activities which most clearly revealed children's loyalties to family and peers.

Whilst attachment theory supports the parents', and particularly the mother's, shaping influence on the child's emotional well-being, yet it does not provide an explanation as to why children persisted in saying that their parents decided what they did at school rather than the teacher. One explanation of this could be that the children associated their parents with school because they took them there and settled them in each morning. Whether this was the reason for the children's response, or not, is perhaps immaterial as the important point was that children indicated by this response that parents were present to them in the classroom, not just emotionally but also pedagogically. This goes beyond the common assumption that home/school links are needed to support the transmission of the school curriculum. It suggests that reception class children actually regard parents, not teachers, as their primary educators.

Indeed there was not much evidence that teachers were seen as emotionally important to the children. The difficult business of forming friendships with peers took precedence over forming relationships with the teacher and despite notions that children make friends easily, this seemed far from the case, with rivalries and alliances played out continually in the newly formed class at St Bede's and, in the case of Abi, with the harsh words from Emma: 'She's got no friends'. Fortunately, however, Paley (1999) writes that children are 'more often kind to each other than unkind', words which were supported by the

Cooper Street teacher's observation, in relation to David, that children's desire to play together was stronger than their desire to compete.

Thus, generally, even when disputes arose over co-operation in play, these were resolved in preference to ending the game altogether. In this way, using Aristotle's *Nicomachean Ethics*, children's friendships can be seen as based on a pleasure which incurs kindness, more to keep the play going than for altruistic ends. Nixon (2004) suggests that to achieve Aristotle's notion of the perfect friendship, pleasure and utility become oriented towards an understanding of each other's best moral interests. This infers that true friendship must take time to develop. Dunn (1993) would concur that children's friendships do inevitably change in line with their social understanding as they grow up. This is not to underestimate their agency in relationships but just to acknowledge that there is a developmental role in the way their relationships change over time.

Therefore, while the project seemed to demonstrate that children's alliances are fluid and in the process of formation, what it also revealed was that children saw these alliances as intrinsic to their survival in the classroom and, to this extent, they relied on the teacher to facilitate the process fairly, through example as well as through specific guidance. The teachers responded to this by using their different pedagogical strengths to talk about building friendships in the classroom. The teachers at St Bede's and Cooper Street used strategies more reliant on cognitive skills than those of the teacher at Allen Road. Nevertheless, for the children, regardless of strategy, all the teachers remained emotionally distant, in comparison to the continuing influence of parents, carers and other family members.

Following this, the third point that the project revealed was that, in the children's eyes, the teacher was predominantly leader, rule-maker and arbiter of the disputes that arose from the business of making and breaking friends with peers. This role presented the most significant challenge to participatory practice in that the teacher's power in this respect was entirely accepted by the children. This explains why pedagogical style has such significance in the development of participatory classroom practices and why participation and learning link. As we saw with the children's adoption of voting in their own play, children imitated the power structures introduced to them by adults. Using the work of Devine (2000), it is possible to identify how children responded to those power structures with resistances built on power structures within their own peer group. Thus, the children were always adapting the adult definitions of the appropriate norms for them. Nevertheless, in a reception class there is bound to be more initial reliance on the adult until these peer relationships are built up.

The teachers at St Bede's and Cooper Street dealt with this challenge by taking on roles as enabler and tutor respectively. While the teacher at St Bede's prioritised children learning to communicate and construct rules, the teacher at Cooper Street aimed to teach co-operation, particularly through the setting up of outdoor play equipment. Despite this, in the larger class at St Bede's, the teacher had limited influence over peer group behaviour, which revealed several examples of exclusivity. This can partly be explained by the lack of nursery in the school, meaning that the children were finding their feet within entirely new groupings, and partly by the more socio-economically privileged context of the school. Thus, at St Bede's, rivalries were constantly being played out and the role of the teacher as enabler appeared to add to the children's need to establish their own hierarchies. Nevertheless, whilst it was possible for an adult visitor to identify which children were being excluded, it was much more difficult to discern who held authority amongst the children and there was a sense in which the culture amongst the children often excluded the adults and remained a secret. Arguably, in her class situation, the teacher at St Bede's may have been advised to extend her practice to the tutor role that Cooper Street's teacher adopted by teaching co-operation in even more active and practical ways.

The fourth main point demonstrated by the project was that structures and routines in teaching practices helped children to resolve disputes and understand other points of view. These structures involved a positive assertion of adult authority in the process of making and implementing rules which protected the vulnerable members of the class, but they also included educative structures such as narratives which invited children to think about the moral issues of classroom life in a way that matched their practical concerns.

The St Bede's teacher's role of facilitator or enabler was built on a practice of making and using stories. This provided the children with structures for negotiating decision-making and was a significant part of her teaching practice which was supported by narrative methods used in the project. Narrative structures allowed children to access multiple viewpoints so that, whereas voting conceded to the majority with an authority which tended to silence the minority, the use of narrative invited children to consider the cases of all participants in a play situation. This revealed that young children are best at sharing decisions about practical issues which directly affect them, rather than about hypothetical situations. However, narratives can bridge this divide by presenting hypothetical situations as real and thus allowing for education of the decision-making process through reflection on the merits of different possibilities.

Narrative was seen to mediate and modify the adult power which was dominant in terms of leadership in the reception classroom. However, there were also other important and related structures used by the teachers that supported children's understandings of decision-making, both individually and collectively. These included the process of voting using tokens which enabled children to experience a sense of agency and its possibilities in the classroom and the use of other props, such as puppets, which the teacher at St Bede's, in particular, relied upon to convey information to the children. Both of these examples provided a ritualised structure which allowed powerful messages to be internalised. The Cooper Street teacher's practice, in particular, relied on familiar songs and routines to provide a sense of structure in the classroom. However, since this was the class which seemed most dependent on adult intervention to sort out disputes, it suggested that strong class routine be regarded in conjunction with less authoritarian models of adult leadership, in order to be participatory. At the same time, however, it is important to maintain authority to educate about fairness and minority, as well as majority, rights.

The project also demonstrated that a reception class of thirty children (St Bede's) was more in need of the teacher to be a rule-maker than a class of eighteen or nineteen children (Allen Road and Cooper Street). Thus, despite the St Bede's teacher's efforts to make the children co-constructors of the classroom rules, the children remained unsettled, to the extent that rules were introduced far more overtly and simply in the subsequent reception class year. However, this teacher's efforts to co-construct rules with the children was part of an attempt to increase the children's participation which was clearly in line with the project's intent. The barriers described in the last paragraph seemed to suggest that the children required a more gradual approach to participation in the complex socio-political area of rule-making than in the more individual and developmental areas of exercising agency and forming alliances.

This gradual approach is characterised by recognition that the adult role is one which determines routines and structures in the classroom, in the sense of the concept of classroom 'habitus' (Bourdieu, 1990). This acknowledgement further merges the notion of participation with that of learning, in that each begins to structure the other and vice versa. This meant that the rational demands of debate were introduced most successfully to the children in a supported manner through the use of routines in the classroom, such as morning circle times at Allen Road, use of puppets and visual means at St Bede's, and outdoor play rotas at Cooper Street and children therefore felt more secure about making decisions about rules. Once again, it was also the structure of narrative which enabled children to think about the implications of their actions. A number of published children's stories, as well as the specially written *Playing Together*, provided examples of situations which could be compared with classroom incidents and arguments. This educative approach to making rules allowed the children to learn about responsibility without having to exercise it in every situation straight away. The St Bede's teacher's experience also suggests that responsibility has to be practised and taught. To support this approach is to give some ground to the theory of mind argument which suggests that young children need developmental time before they can demonstrate appreciation of other points of view. However, most importantly, this is not to say that they are not capable of that appreciation but only, as both Russell (1996) and Dunn and Brown (2001) would concur, that it takes further developmental time to *demonstrate* it.

Participatory projects

In summarising key aspects and challenges of participatory practice in the project, the contribution of the class teachers has been highlighted. Their contribution became all the more dominant in the third term of the project when the two teachers remaining in the project agreed to design participatory projects themselves. These aimed to build on the previous methods which had acted to raise children's awareness of decision-making in their lives. The Allen Road teacher decided to base her participatory project around a process of consultation with children about the end-of-year class trip, while the teacher at St Bede's engaged her children in making a video in order to advise next year's class about school life from a pupil's perspective. The purpose of these projects was to shift the focus from researcher-led to practitioner-led activities and in so doing to embed children's participation more firmly in everyday practices. This aim was evident in a number of ways at Allen Road, with consultation taking place on a number of issues, such as the introduction of a school uniform, attendance at assembly and disciplinary matters as well as the class trip destination. The teacher at Allen Road reported that:

> The children accepted each other's views and were always happy that we implemented the idea or activity that most of the class wanted.

This reflected the interest this class showed in voting systems, which led to this teacher trialling a number of different types, saying:

> We have worked through systems of voting from a 'graph'-type, visual method, a 'putting a pebble in a basket' type system. I also moved onto the coloured cards system that I used last year.

The participatory project at St Bede's was more specific and designed to incorporate the use of the school's video camera. The St Bede's children started the project by talking about and making drawings depicting the aspects of school and class life that they thought were essential for new starters to be aware of. Thus Emma said: 'If you have nobody to play with, ask someone to play' and Keir said: 'don't push or nip people' and 'be careful with people'. The consultation process also allowed children to demonstrate directly their own sense of care and responsibility towards the new children by making comments such as: 'if you fall down we will be kind to you'. The St Bede's teacher commented that listening to children's views in this way 'allowed me to understand the children's attitude to what rules were important to them'. The children's comments seemed to suggest that while they were concerned to impart the rules such as: 'don't go over the white line' and 'don't mess in the toilets', they were even more concerned to reassure the new children that help would be at hand in the new environment, mainly from themselves but also from the classroom assistant. Noticeably, as highlighted by the 'Who Chooses' activity, despite her key role in designing the activity, the teacher was not mentioned as a source of help. This endorses the finding that teachers were not seen by the children as providing emotional support in the classroom. It also, perhaps more importantly, demonstrates these children's growth of independence over the course of the year.

Planning for participation

It has been suggested throughout this account that the most important implications of the project for policy and practice in the reception class pivot on teaching practices and, in particular, the issue of how practices can support children's emotional literacy and ability to communicate and understand other perspectives. This interpretation of the project's work results from the model of participatory democracy that the project explored, one that incurred interaction, communication and negotiation to reach common agreement. In this model, participation incurs both recognition of difference and a process of deliberation, as outlined by Young (2000). However, deliberation in the form of discussion has been identified as a potential difficulty in the context of work with young children, since their verbal negotiation skills are mostly still in formation. Therefore, non-verbal skills, as described in the emphasis on visual and symbolic activities, often provided the best means of getting their message across.

The project also suggested that the transitional aspect of the reception class, from part-time nursery into full-time school life, reinforced the need for teachers to provide familiar forms of expression associated with nursery experiences alongside the introduction of the increasingly complex verbal structures which will eventually inform collective decision-making and children's sense of belonging to a wider school community. It has been argued that these familiar forms, in particular the use of narrative, can form the basis for the development of children's emotional literacy, communication and co-operation in the classroom. This development provides the linchpin, or centre, of this transitional process as it enables children to feel secure enough to form the peer relationships that future negotiation skills are dependent on. This project has suggested that, until children have this sense of security, even fairly competent language skills, as we saw in Tom, are not sufficient for a sense of collective identity as a class member.

However, despite the transitional role of the reception class, it is important not to undermine its importance for participatory work, but conversely to view it as a time of heightened significance for children forging identities, not just as class members but also as learners. In this way, it could also be seen as a metaphor for the position of all children, perpetually in a state of transition to adulthood (James and Prout, 1997). To capture this particular time of significance as learners, a model of participatory teaching practice in the reception class is suggested which encompasses the varying dimensions of individual, social, political and developmental and which builds on the children's perspectives explored in this study. Figure 9.1 shows how these dimensions link to the areas of activity considered in order to achieve a participatory pedagogy. Figure 9.2 then specifies the actual activities used to introduce these areas to children.

The four dimensions of the individual, social, developmental and political indicate the multi-faceted reality of participation with young children which centres on emotion. The four inner areas of activity are equally interdependent and co-exist. Although not specifically identified, communication is inherent in these four areas and particularly nurtured through the games and stories

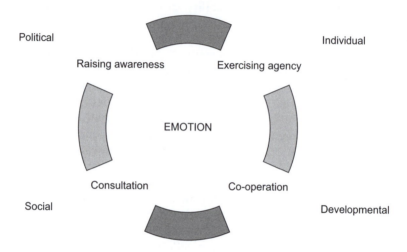

Figure 9.1 A model for participation at the start of school: 1

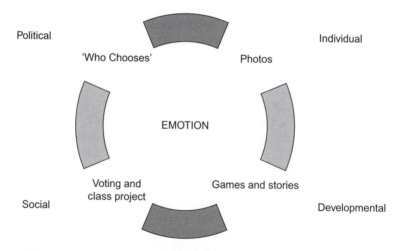

Figure 9.2 A model for participation at the start of school: 2

that lead to co-operation. Since the social and political dimensions are the areas frequently in need of further attention in early education, the corresponding activities in Figure 9.2 are seen as the critical ones which are needed to engage and enhance the participatory abilities of the young child, though they clearly work best in conjunction with attention to the individual and developmental concerns.

Although ironic that the central and pivotal point of emotion in this model was not generally identified by the children as associated with the teacher, this model contends that it was, in fact, the ability of teachers to engage children in an everyday expression of their feelings which the success of other activities was built upon. By providing the structures and activities for children to verbalise their relationships with parents, siblings and each other, the teacher was indeed the central point for the development of children's participation, albeit a hidden facilitator in the process. This peculiarly hidden role is in itself interesting pedagogically as it suggests that, from the children's viewpoint, the process of teaching and learning in the reception class may be more about providing secure structures, including links with home, to allow the new environment and peer group to be negotiated and absorbed, than about providing access to new ideas and adults.

Conclusion

This book attempts to present a rationale, theoretical models and also practical ideas for establishing participatory practice for children in the first year of school. This conjunction of theory and practice is seen as vitally important in both the development of practice with young children and the practitioners who work with them. The book makes these links primarily by relating the questions, methodology and methods of a research project which took place in three reception classes (now often called 'foundation 2' classes) in a city in the north of England. Thus, the findings from the project have been presented in the form of relevant comments, incidents and observations involving the children with references to academic literature to support and debate the points made. The central chapters are framed through questions which concern children when they start school and aim to represent the relevance of democratic participation from their point of view. The final chapter then suggests a schematic approach to planning for participation in the early years at school.

It is suggested that teachers of reception classes should concern themselves with these participatory questions as they oversee a period of transition and initiation to school life that may last beyond the allotted year. Although, hitherto, the start of school has been an area where the issue of children's participation has been neglected, this study contends that it is, in fact, a critical time to reinforce a participatory pedagogy. Thus, the process of settling into school reflects a heightened need for children to grow emotionally, make new friends and begin to understand other perspectives. A participatory approach to teaching and learning means that children will enter into the statutory phase of their education with confidence to build relationships and learn from, as well as alongside, each other.

Since concepts of participation link with those of inclusion and provide a site at which transformations may occur, a participatory pedagogy develops both social inclusion and individual levels of confidence and also enables the possibility of new power relations within pedagogic discourse itself. This is despite an 'institutionalization of knowledge' (Bernstein, 1996, p.45), recognisable in the current high level of state control in curriculum matters.

Teachers, therefore, need to be confident in the strategies they can exercise to help children feel that they belong in the school community. This book suggests that the roles of guide, enabler and tutor all have a place in a participatory pedagogy but that the most supportive atmosphere, to benefit all children in carrying out this work, ideally involves a class of less than twenty children. This allows the role of guide to flourish and thus also the teacher to nourish children's emotional awareness of themselves and each other.

Most importantly, participatory pedagogy should not be viewed as an optional extra but as a vital tool to transform not just children's educational experiences, but also the experience of the adults who work with them. This book is a small contribution to the growing argument for children's viewpoints to be considered fully whatever their age and stage of development. However, it is also, importantly, a request that the often marginal reception class practitioners who work to establish the voice of the child in their classrooms should be given the high status they deserve.

References

Alderson, P. (2000) *Young Children's Rights: Exploring Beliefs, Principles and Practice*. London: Jessica Kingsley.

Allen P. (1990) *Herbert and Harry*. Harmondsworth: Penguin.

Apple, M. (1982) *Education and Power*. Routledge: London.

Barone, T. (1995) 'Persuasive writings, vigilant readings, and reconstructed characters: the paradox of trust in educational storysharing' in Hatch, J., Amos, N. and Wisniewski, R. (eds) *Life History and Narrative*. London: Falmer.

Bauman, Z. (2002) 'Recognition or redistribution? Changing perspectives on the moral order of society' in Lash, S. and Featherstone, M. (eds) *Recognition and Difference*. London: Sage.

Bernstein, B. (1996) *Pedagogy, Symbolic Control and Identity*. London: Taylor & Francis.

Booth, T. and Booth, W. (1996) 'Sounds of silence: narrative research with inarticulate subjects', *Disability and Society*, Vol.11, no. 1, pp.55-70.

Booth, T. (2000) 'Inclusion and exclusion policy in England: Who controls the agenda?' in Armstrong, F. and Barton, L. (eds) *Inclusive Education: Policy, Contexts and Comparative Perspectives*. London: Fulton.

Booth, T., Ainscow, M., Black Hawkins, K., Vaughn, M. and Shaw, L. (2000) *Index for Inclusion: Developing Learning and Participation in Schools*. CSIE: Bristol

Bourdieu, P. (1990) *The Logic of Practice*. Cambridge: Polity.

Bowlby, J. (1969, 1973, 1980) *Attachment and Loss* (3 vols). New York: Basic Harper/Colophon.

Bronfenbrenner, U. (1979) *The Ecology of Human Development: Experiments by Nature and Design*. Massachusetts: Harvard University Press.

Brooker, L. (2002) *Starting School: Young Children Learning Cultures*. Buckingham: OUP.

Bruner, J.S. (1983) *Child's Talk: Learning to Use Language*. Oxford: OUP.

Butler, J. (1997) *Exciteable Speech: A Politics of the Performative*. New York: Routledge.

Cannella, G. and Viruru, R. (2004) *Childhood and Postcolonization*. London: RoutledgeFalmer.

Carr, M. and May, H. (2000) 'Te Whaariki: Curriculum voices' in Penn, H. (ed.) *Early Childhood Services: Theory, Policy and Practice*. Buckingham: OUP.

Carr, W. and Kemmis, S (1986) *Becoming Critical: Education, Knowledge and Action Research*. Lewes: Falmer.

Clark, A. and Moss, P. (2001) *Listening to Children: the Mosaic Approach*. London: National Children's Bureau.

Clifford, J. (1986) 'Introduction: partial truths', in Clifford, J. and Marcus, G. (eds) *Writing Culture: The Poetics and Politics of Ethnography*. Berkeley: University of California Press.

Corsaro, W. (2005) *The Sociology of Childhood*. 2nd edition. London: Sage.

Cuffaro, H. (1995) *Experimenting with the World*. New York: Teachers College Press.

DCSF (1995–2008) *Every Child Matters: Change for Children* [online] @ http://www. everychildmatters.gov.uk/ (accessed Feb 2008).

DCSF (2007) *Statutory Framework for the Early Years Foundation Stage*. London: DCSF.

DfEE (1994) *The Code of Practice on the Identification and Assessment of Children with Special Educational Needs*. London: DfEE.

DfEE (2000) *Curriculum Guidance for the Foundation Stage*. London: DfEE.

DfES (2002) *Birth to Three Matters: A Framework to Support Children in their Earliest Years*. London: DfES.

DfES (2005a) *Key Elements of Effective Practice* (KEEP). London: DfES.

DfES (2005b) *Excellence and Enjoyment: Social and Emotional Aspects of Learning. Getting On and Falling Out: Foundation Stage*. London: DfES.

Dahlberg, G., Moss, P. and Pence, A. (1999) *Beyond Quality in Early Childhood Education and Care: Postmodern Perspectives*. London: Routledge.

Dahlberg, G. and Moss, P. (2005) *Ethics and Politics in Early Childhood Education*. Abingdon: RoutledgeFalmer.

Damon, W. (1990) *The Moral Child: Nurturing Children's Natural Moral Growth*. USA: Free Press.

Davies, L. and Kirkpatrick, G. (2000) *The Euridem Project*. London: Children's Rights Alliance for England.

Denscombe, M. (1998) *The Good Research Guide: for Small Scale Research Projects*. Buckingham: OUP.

Denzin, N.K. (1997) *Interpretive Ethnography*. London: Sage.

Denzin, N.K. (2000) 'The practices and politics of interpretation' in Denzin, N. and Lincoln, Y. (eds) *Handbook of Qualitative Research*: 2nd edn. London: Sage.

De Vries, R. and Zan, B. (1994) *Moral Classrooms, Moral Children*. New York: Teachers College Press.

Devine, D. (2000) 'The Exercise of Power in Children's Experience of School'. *Irish Educational Studies*, Vol. 19, Spring.

Dockett, S. and Perry, B. (2005) 'Starting school in Australia is "a bit safer, a lot easier and more relaxing": issues for families and children from culturally and linguistically diverse backgrounds'. *Early Years*, 25(3), pp.271–81.

Donaldson, M. (1978) *Children's Minds*. Glasgow: Fontana.

Dunn, J. (1993) *Young Children's Close Relationships: Beyond Attachment* (Individual Differences and Development Series, Vol. 4). California: Sage.

Dunn, J. and Brown, J.R. (2001) 'Emotion, pragmatics and social understanding in the preschool years' in Bakhurst, D. and Shanker, S. (eds) *Jerome Bruner: Language, Culture, Self*. London: Sage.

Dyer, P. (2002) 'A "box full of feelings": developing emotional intelligence in a nursery community' in Nutbrown, C. (ed.) *Research Studies in Early Childhood Education*. UK: Trentham.

Einarsdottir, J. (2006) 'From Pre-school to Primary School: When different contexts meet'. *Scandinavian Journal of Educational Research*, Vol. 50, No. 2, April, pp.165–84(20).

Ely, M. (1991) *Doing Qualitative Research: Circles within Circles*. London: Falmer.

Emerson, S. (2001) 'Is it for big children?'. *Coordinate*: issue 82.

Ennison, M. and Smith, P. (2000) *Researching the Visual*. London: Sage.

Fabian, H. and Dunlop, A-W. (2006) 'Outcomes of good transition processes for children entering primary school'. UNESCO paper prepared for the *Education for All Global Monitoring Report 2007, Strong Foundations: Early Childhood Care and Education.*

Farquhar, S. (2005) 'Family and identity' in Mason, M. (ed.) Philosophy of Education Society of Australasia 34th Annual Conference: *Critical Thinking and Learning: Values, Concepts and Issues.* Hong Kong: PESA.

Foucault, M. (1972) *The Archaeology of Knowledge,* trans. A. M. Sheridan Smith. London: Tavistock.

Foucault, M (1979) *Discipline and Punish. The Birth of the Prison.* New York: Vintage; Random House.

Foucault, M. (1980) *Power/Knowledge: Selected Interviews and other Writings, 1972–1977,* ed. C. Gordon. London: Harvester Wheatsheaf.

Foucault, M. (1982) 'The subject and power' in Dreyfus H. and Rabinow P. (eds) *Michel Foucault: Beyond Structuralism and Hermeneutics.* Brighton: Harvester Press.

Fountain, S. (1990) *Learning Together: Global Education 4–7.* Godalming: WWF.

Fraser, N. (1995) 'From redistribution to recognition? Dilemmas of justice in a "post-socialist" age'. *New Left Review* 212: 68–93.

Freire, P. (1970) *Pedagogy of the Oppressed.* New York: Seabury.

Freire, P. (1972) *Cultural Action for Freedom*: London, Penguin.

Freud, S. (1914) 'On narcissism' in Strachey, J. (ed and trans.) *The Standard Edition of the Complete Psychological Works of Sigmund Freud.* London: Hogarth Press

Fulcher, G. (1989) *Disabling Policies? A Comparative Approach to Education Policy and Disability.* London: Falmer.

Gilligan, C. (1988) 'New images of self in relationship' in Gilligan, C., Ward, J.V. and Taylor, J.M. (eds) *Mapping the Moral Domain.* New York: Harvard.

Gilligan, C. and Wiggins, G. (1988) 'The origins of morality in early childhood relationships' in Gilligan, C., Ward, J.V., and Taylor, J.M. (eds) *Mapping the Moral Domain.* New York: Harvard.

Glass, R. (2001) 'On Paulo Freire's philosophy of praxis and the foundations of liberation education'. *Educational Researcher*, March. [online] @ http://www.aera.net/uploadedFiles/Journals_and_Publications/Journals/Educational_Researcher/3002/AERA3002_Glass.pdf (accessed May 2008).

Griffiths, M. (1995) *Feminisms and the Self: The Web of Identity.* London: Routledge.

Habermas, J. (1984) *The Theory of Communicative Action*, Vol. 1. Cambridge, Polity Press.

Habermas, J. (1987) *The Theory of Communicative Action*, Vol. 2. Cambridge, Polity Press.

Hart, R. (1992) 'Children's participation: from tokenism to citizenship', Series: *Innocenti Essays*, no.4. Florence: UNICEF

Haynes, J. and Murris, K. (2000) 'Thinking for themselves'. *Coordinate* 79, Winter.

Hoffman, M. (1977) 'Sex differences in empathy and related behaviors'. *Psychological Bulletin*, 84(4), pp.712–22.

Holt, J. (1975) *Escape from Childhood: The Needs and Rights of Children.* Harmondsworth: Penguin.

Honneth, A. (2002) 'Recognition or redistribution?' in Lash, S. and Featherstone, M. (eds) *Recognition and Difference.* London: Sage.

Hutter, H. (1978) *Politics as Friendship: The Origins of Classical Notions of Politics in the Theory and Practice of Friendship.* Waterloo, Ontario: Wilfred Laurier University Press.

Jackson, M. (1982) 'Making sense of school' in Pollard, A. (ed.) *Children and their Primary Schools.* Lewes: Falmer.

James, A. and Prout, A. (eds) (1997) *Constructing and Reconstructing Childhood*. London: Falmer.

James, A., Jenks, C. and Prout, A. (eds) (1998) *Theorising Childhood*. Cambridge: Polity.

Jeffcoate, R. (1980) *Positive Images Towards a Multi-racial Curriculum*. London: Writers and Readers Publishing Cooperative.

Kemmis, S. and McTaggart, R. (2000) 'Participatory action research' in Denzin, N. and Lincoln, Y. (eds) *Handbook of Qualitative Research*. 2nd edn. London: Sage.

Kirby. P., Lanyon, C., Cronin, C. and Sinclair, R. (2003) *Building a Culture of Participation*. London: DfES.

Kjorholt, A-T., Moss, P. and Clark, A. (2005) 'Beyond listening: Future prospects' in Clark, A., Kjorholt, A.T., and Moss, P. (eds) *Beyond Listening: Children's Perspectives on Early Childhood Services*. Bristol: Policy Press.

La Fontaine, J.S. (1979) *Sex and Age as Principles of Social Differentiation*. London: Academic Press.

Lacan, J. (1977) *Ecrits: A Selection,* trans. A. Sheridan. London: Tavistock.

Lather, P. (1991) *Getting Smart: Feminist Research and Pedagogy with/in the Postmodern*. London: Routledge.

Lewis, C., Freeman, N.H., Kyriakidou, C., Maridaki-Kossotaki, K. and Berridge, D.M. (1996) 'Social influences on false belief access: specific sibling influences or general apprenticeship?' *Child Development*, 67: pp.2930–47.

Malaguzzi *et al.*, (2005) *Catalogue of the exhibit: The hundred languages of children*. Reggio Emilia, Italy: Reggio Children.

Marcus, G. (1994) 'What comes (just) after "post"?' in Denzin, N. and Lincoln, Y. (eds) *Handbook of Qualitative Research*. Thousand Oaks, CA.: Sage.

Mosley, J. and Sonnet, H. (2005) *Better Behaviour through Golden Time*. Cambridge: LDA.

Moss, P. (1998) 'Adopting a new approach'. *Coordinate*, January.

Moss, P. (2001) 'Listen in'. *Nursery World*, 5 July.

Moss, P., Clark, A. and Kjorholt, A-T. (2005) *Beyond Listening: Children's Perspectives on Early Childhood Services*. Bristol: Policy Press.

Moyles, J., Adams, S. and Musgrove, A. (2002) *SPEEL: Study of Pedagogical Effectiveness on Early Learning*. London: DfES.

New Zealand Ministry of Education (1996) *Te Whaariki*. Wellington: Learning Media.

New Zealand Ministry of Education (2002) *Pathways to the future. Nga huarahi arataki*. Wellington: Learning Media.

Nixon, J. (2001) 'Imagining Ourselves into Being: conversing with Hannah Arendt'. *Pedagogy, Culture and Society*: 9, 2.

Nixon, J. (2004) 'Learning the language of deliberative democracy' in Walker, M. and Nixon, J. (eds) *Reclaiming Universities from a Runaway World*. Buckingham: OUP.

Nixon, J., Martin, J., McKeown, P. and Ranson, S. (eds) (1996) *Encouraging Learning*. Buckingham: OUP.

OECD, Directorate for Education (2004) *Five Curriculum Outcomes*: *Starting Strong: Curricula and Pedagogies in Early Childhood Education and Care*. [online] @ http//www.oecd.org/dataoecd/23/36/31672150.pdf (accessed Aug 2008).

O'Kane, C. (2000) 'The development of participatory techniques' in Christensen, P. and James, A. (eds), *Research with Children*. London: Routledge.

Oliver, M. (1996) *Understanding Disability: From Theory to Practice*. Basingstoke: Palgrave.

Osler, A. (ed.) (2000) *Citizenship and Democracy in Schools*. Stoke: Trentham.

Paley, V.G. (1999) *The Kindness of Children*. London: Harvard University Press.

Penn, H. (1998) 'You've got a friend'. *Co-ordinate,* January.

Phillips, A. (1993) *Democracy and Difference*. Cambridge: Polity Press.

Priestley, M. (1999) 'Discourse and identity: Disabled children in mainstream High Schools' in Corker, M. and French, S. (eds) *Disability Discourse*. Buckingham: OUP.

Pritchard, M. (1996) *Reasonable Children: Moral Education and Moral Learning*. Kansas: University Press of Kansas.

Prosser, J. (1998) (ed.) *Image-based Research*. London: Falmer.

Prout, A. and James, A. (1997) 'A new paradigm for the sociology of childhood? Provenance, promise and problems' in James, A. & Prout, A. (eds) *Constructing and Reconstructing Childhood*. London: Falmer.

Qualifications and Curriculum Authority (QCA) (1998) *Education for Citizenship and the Teaching of Democracy in Schools: Final Report of the Advisory Group on Citizenship*, (The Crick Report) 22 Sept. London: QCA.

QCA (2002) *Citizenship at Key Stages 1-4: Guidance on Assessment, Recording and Reporting*. London: QCA.

QCA (2004) *Religious Education: The Non-statutory National Framework*. London: QCA.

Rinaldi, C (2005) *In Dialogue with Reggio Emilia*. London: Routledge

Road, N. (2004) 'Are equalities an issue?' in *Listening as a Way of Life*. London: NCB.

Rogoff, B. (2003) *The Cultural Nature of Human Development*. Oxford: Oxford University Press.

Rorty, R. (1998) *Achieving our Country: Leftist Thought in Twentieth-century America*. Series: The William E. Massey, Sr. lectures in the history of American civilisation. Cambridge, Mass: Harvard University Press.

Russell, J. (1996) *Agency: Its Role in Mental Development*. Landon: Taylor & Francis.

Schon, D. (1983) *The Reflective Practitioner: How Professionals Think in Action*. London: Temple Smith.

Selman, R.L. (1980) *The Growth of Interpersonal Understanding: Developmental and Clinical Analyses*. London: Academic Press.

Sevenhuijsen, S. (1998) *Citizenship and the Ethics of Care: Feminist Considerations on Justice, Morality and Politics*. London: Routledge.

Sheridan, S. and Pramling Samuelsson, I. (2001) 'Children's conceptions of participation and influence in Pre-school: A perspective on pedagogical quality'. *Contemporary Issues in Early Childhood*, Vol. 2, No. 2.

Shulman, L. (2002) 'A perspective on teacher knowledge' in Pollard, A. (ed.) *Readings for Reflective Teaching*. London: Continuum.

Simmel, G. (1950) 'The stranger', in Kurt Wolff (trans.) *The Sociology of Georg Simmel*. New York: Free Press, pp.402–408.

Siraj-Blatchford, I., Sylva, K., Muttock, S., Gilden, R. and Bell, D. (2002) *Researching Effective Pedagogy in the Early Years*. London: DfES.

Skrtic, T. (1991) *Behind Special Education*. Colorado: Love.

Smith, A.B., and May, H. (2006) 'Early childhood care and education in Aotearoa- New Zealand' in Melhuish E. and Petrogiannis K. (eds) *Early Childhood Care and Education: International Perspectives*, pp. 95–114. London: Routledge.

Stanton, M. (1983) *Outside the Dream: Lacan and French Styles of Psychoanalysis*. London: Routledge and Kegan Paul.

Sylva, K., Melhuish, E., Sammons, P., Siraj-Blatchford, I. and Taggart, B. (2004) *The Effective Provision of Pre-School Education {EPPE} Project. Final Report. A Longitudinal Study funded by the DfES 1997–2004* [online] @ http://www.surestart.gov.uk/_doc/P0001378.pdf (accessed Aug 2008).

Tedlock, B. (2000) 'Ethnography and ethnographic representation', in Denzin, N. and Lincoln, Y. (eds) *Handbook of Qualitative Research.* 2nd edn. London: Sage.

Usher, R. and Edwards, R. (1994) *Postmodernism and Education.* London: Routledge.

UN (1989) Convention on the Rights of the Child [online] @: http://www. ohchr.org (accessed July 2006).

Viruru, R. (2007) 'Resisting resistance in postcolonial theory: implications for the study of childhood'. *International Journal of Equity and Innovation in Early Childhood*, Vol. 5, No. 1.

Walkerdine, V. (1988) *The Mastery of Reason.* London: Routledge.

Williams, R. (1958) *Culture and Society.* London and New York: Columbia University Press.

Woodhead, M. (1999) 'Towards a global paradigm for research into early childhood education'. *European Early Childhood Education Research Journal*, Vol. 7, No.1.

Woodhead, M. (2000) 'Children's rights and children's development: rethinking the paradigm' *Ghent Papers on Children's Rights*, No. 6. Ghent: Children's Rights Centre.

Young, I. (2000) *Inclusion and Democracy.* Oxford: OUP.

Index

eBooks

eBooks – at www.eBookstore.tandf.co.uk

A library at your fingertips!

eBooks are electronic versions of printed books. You can store them on your PC/laptop or browse them online.

They have advantages for anyone needing rapid access to a wide variety of published, copyright information.

eBooks can help your research by enabling you to bookmark chapters, annotate text and use instant searches to find specific words or phrases. Several eBook files would fit on even a small laptop or PDA.

NEW: Save money by eSubscribing: cheap, online access to any eBook for as long as you need it.

Annual subscription packages

We now offer special low-cost bulk subscriptions to packages of eBooks in certain subject areas. These are available to libraries or to individuals.

For more information please contact
webmaster.ebooks@tandf.co.uk

We're continually developing the eBook concept, so keep up to date by visiting the website.

www.eBookstore.tandf.co.uk